LOON

JACK McLEAN

LOON

a marine story

BALLANTINE BOOKS TRADE PAPERBACKS / NEW YORK

2010 Ballantine Books Trade Paperback Edition

Copyright © 2009 by Jack McLean
Title-page photograph copyright © 2009 by AP Images
Map copyright © 2010 by Mapping Specialists, Ltd.

Published in the United States by Ballantine Books, an imprint of The Random House Publishing Group, a division of Random House, Inc., New York.

BALLANTINE and colophon are trademarks of Random House, Inc.

Originally published in hardcover and in slightly different form in the United States by Presidio Press, an imprint of The Random House Publishing Group, a division of Random House, Inc., in 2009.

Grateful acknowledgment is made to Oakfield Avenue Music and John Cale Music, Inc., for permission to reprint lyrics from "I Believe," written by Lou Reed and John Cale. Copyright © Oakfield Avenue Music and John Cale Music. Copyright © Metal Machine Music and John Cale Music, Inc. U.S. and Canadian rights for Oakfield Avenue Music administered and controlled by Spirit One Music (BMI). World excluding U.S. and Canadian rights controlled and administered by EMI Music Publishing, Ltd. International copyright secured. Used by permission. All rights reserved.

Library of Congress Cataloging-in-Publication Data
McLean, Jack
Loon: a Marine story / Jack McLean.
p. cm.
ISBN 978-0-345-51016-7
1. Vietnam War, 1961–1975—Personal narratives, American. 2. McLean, Jack, 1947– 3. Marines—United States—Biography. 4. United States Marine Corps—Biography. I. Title.
DS559.5.M4185   2009
959.704'345092—dc22

www.ballantinebooks.com

Book design by Casey Hampton

147429898

For my mother,
Martha Lamb McLean

PREFACE

Valerie Solanas took the elevator
Got off at the 4th floor
She pointed the gun at Andy saying
"You cannot control me anymore"

I believe there's got to be some retribution
I believe an eye for an eye is elemental
I believe that something's wrong if she's alive right now
                    —"I Believe" by Lou Reed and John Cale

ON THE AFTERNOON OF JUNE 3, 1968, IN NEW YORK City, Valerie Solanas, a rejected actress and a cult hero to a small segment of postmodern quasi-feminists, shot popular artist Andy Warhol three times in the chest at the Factory, his New York studio at 231 East Forty-seventh Street. She worked there occasionally. Solanas was the founder and sole member of a group named SCUM (Society for Cutting Up Men). When she was arrested the following day, she said, "He had too much control over my life." She was later found to be insane and was confined to a mental institution for six years. Warhol initially was

pronounced dead, but, after a desperate heart massage, he survived.

An hour later, sixty-five blocks uptown, at the magnificent
Cathedral Church of Saint John the Divine on Amsterdam Avenue, history professor Richard Hofstadter was giving the Columbia University commencement address to what remained of
a ragged collection of several thousand angry seniors. Most had
walked out to protest America's growing involvement in the war
in Vietnam. Fittingly, Hofstadter's subject was violence, more
specifically the effect that the rapidly escalating war in Vietnam
was having on the fabric of American society:

> This misconceived venture in Vietnam has inflamed our stu-
> dents, undermined their belief in our political process, and
> convinced them that violence is the order of the day. I share
> their horror at this war. The deep alienation it has inflicted
> on young Americans is one of the staggering costs of the
> Vietnam undertaking. While this war has toppled a presi-
> dent, its full effects on our national life have yet to be reck-
> oned.

The following day, June 4, 1968, a dozen United States Marine Corps CH-46 helicopters, two minutes apart, lifted slowly
off the ground from their base at Quang Tri, Vietnam, and ac-
celerated at an extreme angle to the west. Their destination was
Camp Carroll. The mission was to pick up the one hundred
eighty boys of Charlie Company and transport them, fifteen air-
minutes, to the last piece of earth that many would ever see. On
a map, it was called Hill 672, part of a rugged series of foothills
southwest of Khe Sanh that protected the borders of both North
Vietnam and Laos. For those of us who survived the coming
three days of horror, it would become forever known as LZ
Loon, or simply Loon.

On the following evening, June 5, 1968, Bobby Kennedy was
shot at the Ambassador Hotel in Los Angeles by Sirhan Sirhan,
a twenty-four-year-old Jordanian national. Kennedy, a native of

my hometown of Brookline, Massachusetts, had enrolled at Harvard University only to drop out after several years to serve his country in the navy during World War II. To some, he was the best hope for a country that seemed to be in a spiraling decline. To many, his assassination was the last, unbelievably violent, straw. Among the stunned individuals that day were a growing number of the then 537,482 American boys serving in Vietnam who were fighting the very war that America was abandoning. A master politician like his brother, Kennedy knew that his best chance to win in November hinged on his opposition to the war in Vietnam, and so oppose he did, with a fervor that left Minnesota senator Eugene McCarthy and other early political leaders of the antiwar movement far behind.

Robert F. Kennedy was forty-two years old. He died the following morning, on June 6, 1968.

Those of us in Charlie Company who survived LZ Loon would not hear the news for another week.

Many of us died that day as well.

NORTHERN I CORPS, SOUTH VIETNAM, 1968
CHARLIE COMPANY OUTPOSTS AND
OPERATIONAL AREAS

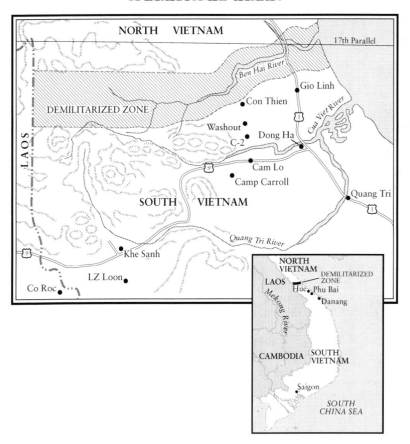

LOON

1

JUNE 6, 1968.

It had already been a long day, and dawn had yet to break.

On his hands and knees, Bill Matthews scampered up over loose rocks and jumped into Bill Negron's hole. Out of breath, he gasped, "They're diggin' in. They're right in front of my hole, Skipper. I can hear 'em. They're all over the fuckin' place."

"Now, hang on, marine. Cool it. Catch your breath. Who's digging in and where?" Negron was calm.

"The gooks, for chrissake. The NVA, just like they did at Con Thien before they came through the wire, and, in case you haven't noticed, we ain't got no fuckin' wire . . . sir." Matthews caught his slight sarcasm and tried to temper it.

Negron grabbed his radio handset and called over to the 3rd Platoon. "Charlie Three, this is Charlie Six Actual, do you read me? Over."

"Six, this is Three. Go."

"Three, this is Six Actual." Negron was gripping the handset ever more tightly so as not to miss a word. "Is everything cool down there?"

"That's a negative, Six. I think the visiting team has arrived and is getting ready for the kickoff. Over."

"Charlie One," "Charlie Two," and "Charlie Three" were
the radio call signs of the platoons that comprised C Company,
1st Battalion, 4th Regiment, 3rd Marine Division. Charlie Six
was the company commander, in this case, Captain William P.
Negron. The "Actual" meant Negron himself as opposed to a
designee, such as his radio operator.

A brief radio silence was broken by a call from the 1st Platoon. "Charlie Six, this is Charlie One. We've got company
about five-zero meters out. Over."

"One, this is Six Actual. Roger that. Give me an azimuth.
Over."

Negron was looking for the exact coordinates of the reported
activity so he could direct 60 mm mortar fire to the area.

"Six, this is One. Wait out . . . Six, this is One—one-five mils
magnetic. Over."

"Incoming!" came the call from the near side of the perimeter.

The ensuing explosion was followed by yet another call.
"Grasshopper Charlie Six, this is Grasshopper Six Actual.
Things sound kinda rough up there for you. Give me a sit rep.
Over." "Grasshopper Six Actual" was the call sign for our bat-
talion commander, Lieutenant Colonel James H. MacLean (no
relation to me).

"Grasshopper Six, this is Charlie Six Actual. We are in the
V ring. Surrounded by unhappy gooks. Send water, ammo, air,
and arty. *Now*. Over."

"Charlie Six, this is Grasshopper Six. I read you loud and
clear. What's your body count? Over."

"Grasshopper Six, be advised that I've lost an entire offensive football team and one baseball team. I'm too busy killing
'em to count 'em. I'll be back when it's quieter. Over."

"Roger that, Charlie Six. Groceries and goodies are on the
way. Over and out."

The brief radio silence was followed by an urgent whisper on
another radio that was barely audible.

"Charlie Six, this is Charlie Three. Over."

It was the voice of 3rd Platoon radio operator Mitchell calling from LZ Loon across the ravine.

"This is Six. Go," replied Terry Tillery. Tillery was Charlie Company's radio operator, and never far from Negron's side.

"Six, they're coming at you. We can see it from here. They're all over your fuckin' perimeter and they are coming at you. Over."

Negron grabbed the handset from Tillery.

"Three, this is Six Actual, do you read me? Over."

"Roger that, Skipper." Mitchell was out of breath and scared.

"Three, can you give me their grid coordinates. Give me some numbers so I can lay some lumber on them."

With that, two 122 mm rockets screamed over the perimeter, followed by a volley of incoming grenades, mortars, and small-arms fire. The ground attack had begun.

"Here they come!" someone screamed.

"Gooks in the perimeter!" came the cry from the 2nd Platoon lines.

"Gooks in the perimeter!" came the cry again, now from the Delta Company lines. Delta marines were engaged in hand-to-hand combat with the enemy.

Negron, observing the assault, looked calmly to John Camacho, the artillery forward observer, and gave a sullen nod. "Do it. Do it now." Camacho picked up his handset and called the rear. Negron then turned to Tillery, his radio operator, and said, "Pass the word. Get everybody in a hole. *Now.*"

"All stations on this net, this is Charlie Six," Tillery stated. "Be advised we are calling them in on us. Repeat, calling them in on us. Pass the word. Get down. Now. Over."

Negron, Camacho, and Tillery slid into a small command bunker they'd dug out the night before. Had there been time, they'd have dug it a mile deeper.

Minutes passed. Camacho got final confirmation of the coming artillery bombardment from the rear and, eschewing the radio, yelled "ON THE WAY!" and leapt back into the bunker.

Around the perimeter, from hole to hole, came the cries of "ON THE WAY!" and "FIRE IN THE HOLE!" At once, we all got small.

Camacho, on Negron's order, had instructed our supporting artillery to fire directly onto our position. We prayed like hell that none of the rounds fell directly into any of our fighting holes. We had little choice. The NVA had broken through our lines in several places and were now inside our perimeter.

The following seconds passed in near silence but for the sporadic crack of an enemy AK-47 rifle. Then it came. The air at once was filled with exploding artillery, flying shrapnel, and screaming boys. Their boys. The artillery air bursts, ordered by Camacho, had caught the enemy in the open. Instead of exploding on impact, the artillery had been fused to ignite in the air above the battlefield. It was slaughter.

With the last explosion, we leapt from the safety of our holes to reinforce the lines and ensure that every NVA soldier who had penetrated the perimeter was dead.

They were scattered everywhere, and they were all very dead.

2

KIDS LIKE ME DIDN'T GO TO VIETNAM.

I was comfortably reared in an upper-middle-class suburb, and my young life was directly out of *The Adventures of Ozzie and Harriet*. From earliest memory, my parents said that I could be anything I wanted to be. Teachers, neighbors, and peers reinforced this ideal. Perhaps I might become a lawyer like my father or an artist like my mother. I developed a strong interest in architecture. I dreamed of creating fabulous modern buildings to rival those of Le Corbusier or Frank Lloyd Wright. Anything was possible, for I was to become the beneficiary of the best education that money and influence could secure.

The fathers of my generation had gone from surviving the Great Depression to crushing the Japanese and saving Europe. They came home with hard-earned pride and the promise to renew their interrupted lives.

The first act for most of our fathers upon returning home was to make us—millions of us, in unprecedented numbers. I was born on May 26, 1947, in the earliest wave of what became known as the great postwar baby boom. In a few short years, we would be more than half of the American population. The society that spawned us, however, was unprepared for our arrival.

Each school year, our class was twice the size of the year before. Classrooms were bursting. Elementary schools could not be built fast enough. Town budgets were strained.

Still, we were a generation with limitless opportunity. America was flowering with unprecedented wealth. For the first time since the Great Depression of the 1930s, the national economy was on a solid steady rise. The newly passed GI Bill of Rights afforded every returning veteran the opportunity to attend college, largely at the government's expense. Skilled jobs were being created to meet the growing demand. Homes could not be built fast enough. Suburbs sprang up throughout the country to supply affordable housing for the burgeoning families. With the jobs and the homes came families and a demand for consumer goods and services that had been unimagined before the war. There grew an expectation that each family would have a car, washing machine, television set, refrigerator, and telephone. Unemployment fell to an unprecedented 2 percent of the workforce.

All was not perfect, however. Although we emerged from World War II as the sole nuclear power, the Soviet Union and others soon joined the club. We were good. The Russians were bad. The looming specter of a nuclear holocaust became vivid in our everyday lives, and many families built home fallout shelters. We practiced "duck and cover" drills under our desks at school. Aboveground atomic testing became routine throughout the world.

In 1950, we were brought into war on the Korean peninsula to combat Communism for the first time. It ended in a divided stalemate three years later. Three years after that, at the Geneva Convention, the remote Southeast Asian country of Vietnam was similarly divided after the defeat of the French colonialists. There was a growing resolve throughout the decade that Communism was evil and must be fought at every turn.

The United States and the Soviet Union built atomic bombs in staggering numbers and aimed them at each other. We maintained huge numbers of troops in Germany, Japan, and Korea to deter the looming threat. To maintain the troop levels, a compulsory draft required all boys in good physical health of eighteen years and older to serve a minimum of two years in the military. Those in school, whether high school or college, were deferred until they graduated or dropped out. That was the law. It applied to all and had been in place since before we were born. From an early age, consequently, we all knew we would have to serve. Yet, in spite of the threat, we grew up with privilege that was unimagined even a generation before. Many became the first in their families to attend college.

Our new generation became defined on the steps of the United States Capitol on January 20, 1961. There in the cold and the snow stood the young, vibrant John Fitzgerald Kennedy, the thirty-fifth president of the United States—his right hand gently resting on the Bible held by his wife, Jacqueline. He extolled service and sacrifice.

Ask not what your country can do for you; ask what you can do for your country.

Thanks to Kennedy, there was still a strong feeling that one individual could make a difference in the world. Millions of young Americans enthusiastically heeded his words and set forth to execute the Kennedy vision. My cousin Mike Ingraham became a freedom rider, one of thousands of Northerners to bus to the Southern United States in support of Dr. Martin Luther King, Jr., and the burgeoning civil rights movement. My brother, Don, entered the newly formed Peace Corps after college in 1964 and spent the next two years teaching school in northern Thailand.

One of the less noticed initiatives of the Kennedy administration occurred shortly after his inauguration when he quietly began to approve the deployment of American advisers to a remote corner of Southeast Asia called Vietnam. This number slowly edged upward until August 7, 1964, when, at the direction of President Johnson, Congress passed the Gulf of Tonkin Resolution, which granted the president broad discretion in Southeast Asia. The resolution was passed in response to the alleged attack on an American vessel in the Gulf of Tonkin by the

North Vietnamese. By December 1965, there were nearly two
hundred thousand American troops in Vietnam. Most of them
were United States Marines. By the time I arrived, there were
nearly half a million American ground forces in Vietnam, and
President Johnson was more determined than ever to achieve an
unconditional victory.

There would be no turning back.

My life was unremarkable, though it was one of privilege.
Brought up in the New York City suburb of Summit, New Jersey, I learned to swim at the YMCA and attended Brayton Elementary School and Summit Junior High. Our family car was
a 1956 Ford Country Squire station wagon. My parents reluctantly purchased our first television set in 1953. During the
spring, I played pickup baseball at Memorial Field. My idol was
Mickey Mantle. I took trumpet and piano lessons, went to dancing class, and did well in school. I had a paper route delivering
the *Newark Evening News*. Everybody liked me, and I liked
everybody.

I was a most agreeable child.

By the sixth grade I was a minor rock and roll idol in my own
mind, writing music and performing at school talent shows. I
had an interest in baseball, Buddy Holly, and girls.

I worshipped my brother, Don, who was six years my senior.
His every move was watched, his every word hung upon as ultimate wisdom and truth. I wanted to be just like him. He was
sent away to boarding school when I was nine and thereafter returned only for vacations during the school year. I lived for the
small bits of attention that I was able to garner from him after
that.

My older sister, Ruth, was especially dear to me. She was
closer in age and a rebel, particularly when it came to our parents. While I was trying my best to please them, Ruthie was constantly pushing the edge. I adored her and was admiring of both

her directness and her ability to live life on her own terms, usually against high odds.

Barby, six years younger than I, felt that she missed the experiences that the older three shared and was doomed to be brought up in a separate family as an only child. That wasn't true, of course. We older three had so worn Mom and Dad down that there was no negative energy left for Barb. Like our mother, she was artistic, expressive, and sensitive.

Summers were spent with extended family on a large lake in southern Quebec, near the small border town that spawned my mother. Childhood times at the lake were the happiest of my life. Summer days passed like years.

Although we knew some boys who went into the military after high school or college, it was not all that common. Most were deferred from the draft by attending high school and college. Those who did serve were normally sent to Korea, Germany, or Japan for a year and then quietly came home. If you were called, you served.

In the fifties, it was that simple.

The change began in the 1960s. The escalating war in Vietnam played a role, as did a feeling of privilege and entitlement among many in the baby boom generation. Although our fathers and perhaps even older brothers had served in the military, many of our number increasingly felt that service was an inconvenience that we need not endure.

Yet by the time the first wave of baby boomers entered college in 1965, the war in Vietnam was turning hot, and military service—*combat* military service—was becoming an increasing reality for the millions of boys who were nearing draft age. Avoiding war service reached an art form. Sympathetic physicians were called on to overstate physical infirmities.

President Bill Clinton tied his local draft board in knots with verbal hijinks and did not serve. President George W. Bush used family connections to gain assignment to a local National Guard unit, which was at the time a sure way to avoid going to Vietnam.

By staying in school, manipulating local draft boards, and exercising political influence, the country's educated class was able to avoid war service almost completely. Thereby, the coming war in Vietnam would be the first American conflict fought almost exclusively by the lower classes of American society. Their available numbers were enormous, and they had neither the resources to avoid the draft nor the inclination to do so.

With high school nearing for me, my father planned that, like my brother, Don, I would attend boarding school. Donny went to Deerfield Academy in western Massachusetts and had an agreeable experience. Dad had attended Phillips Academy in Andover, Massachusetts. To him, Andover was an obvious choice. He was also on the board of trustees. I was ever eager to please. The following fall I arrived at Andover.

On a rainy mid-September evening in 1961, four months after my fourteenth birthday, I sat in the large auditorium in Andover's George Washington Hall along with the two hundred other incoming boys.

Included in the select group that day was George W. Bush, a future president of the United States. We would spend the next three years together.

Andover had long prided itself on its ability and desire to attract "youth from every quarter." Looking about the hall that evening, however, it was apparent that the quarter that included white upper-class males was predominant. Each boy wore a jacket and tie. We ranged in age from fourteen to seventeen years old. Had shoes been visible, one would have seen only Bass penny loafers.

The headmaster and the dean of students were seated alone on the left side of the large curtained stage of George Washington Hall facing the sea of well-scrubbed and attentive new faces that included mine. Before them stood a single lectern upon which hung the official seal of Phillips Academy.

Summit Junior High School did not have an official seal.

I was to struggle badly during my first year and was forced to repeat it. Consequently, for the next five years, I would see the headmaster and the dean of students in the same two chairs at exactly the same place twice a week at each all-school assembly. They had their act down. I didn't sense that they were as curious about us as we were about them.

The headmaster spoke, reinforcing the gravity of our mission.

"You are tomorrow's leaders today," he began.

The school mottoes were put forth—*finis origine pendet* (the end depends upon the beginning) and *non sibi* (not for self). Fortunately, my parents had decided that I would take Latin. Apparently, it would be needed.

Then the dean of students spoke. "You will adhere to a strict set of rules."

One of his favorite rules was "abjure the hypotenuse" (stay on the paved paths; don't cut across the grass). "Abjure"? My vocabulary was going to need work. This was a serious place.

Socially, I adapted well to Andover. We wore jackets and ties, attended chapel every morning, and lived in dormitories. There were no parents. I liked the structure and, as it turned out, the discipline as well. It was a place of history, purpose, and tradition.

Coming as I did from a rigid, conservative upbringing, I responded well to history, purpose, and tradition. My parents knew that Andover would reinforce this in me as it had done for generations of boys before me.

They couldn't imagine at the time that this same reasoning would lead me to enlist in the United States Marine Corps five years later.

3

THE YEAR WAS 1966.

The old Victorian house was silent.

Home from Andover near the end of spring break, I was more accustomed to the raucous activity of a dormitory. Outside, a bus ground its gears up High Street, the sound muted by heavy storm windows and thick rhododendron bushes. The late-afternoon air was cold with not even a hint of the spring to come. Dark clouds coursed across the winter sky. Inside, the once glowing embers were slowly dying in the parlor fireplace. The occasional hissing and clanging of the radiators had ceased.

I was alone.

The occasional moments of quiet that I felt in the big house could be disconcerting. My family had moved from New Jersey to Brookline, Massachusetts, the previous year. I had never really spent time in this house except during vacations and weekend stopovers. Consequently, there were neither real memories—fond or otherwise—nor old neighbors eager to catch a glimpse of my rare visit home.

On the front hall table sat the day's mail, carefully deposited in the gold tray by my mother. As was her custom, she had picked up the pile from the vestibule floor below the front door mail slot, taken that which applied to her, and left the balance for my sister, my father, and me to sort through. At the top of the tidy stack was a letter addressed to me.

I stopped.

Two things immediately and simultaneously caught my eye—the origin of the letter was the office of admissions at Colby College, and the envelope was thin.

I was about to commence the spring term of my senior year. I was taking five courses and was in serious danger of passing only two. It had been an exceptionally rigorous *five* years for me at Andover. College admission was a concern but was darkly overshadowed by the prospect that I might not even graduate from high school. I had passively applied to five colleges, had already been rejected by four, and was now waiting fatalistically for the last. It appeared that moment was nigh.

Acceptance letters came in fat envelopes.

Everyone agreed that I was a bright boy. When I was ten, I could instantly recompute a baseball average with each at bat but was somehow unable to translate such talent to academics. That I was able to survive five long years at Andover was a testament both to my resilience and to the feeling among the faculty that I was a good kid who really was trying.

I picked up the envelope and slowly pulled open the flap. As suspected, I was now oh-for-five.

Surprisingly, relief enveloped me.

My clouded future began to clear. I hadn't wanted to go to college right away, and, having given the process an honest try, it was apparent now that college didn't want me either. No doubt the powers at Andover would put their full efforts into getting me in *somewhere,* but I didn't want to go somewhere just for the sake of going to college. To me it seemed . . . well . . . sort of dishonest.

The next several years would find me elsewhere.

There would be two issues that I would have to face should I decide not to go to college. The year was 1966. There was a draft. If you were eighteen or older, male, and of sound body and mind, it was your duty—indeed it was the law—to serve the country in the military for a minimum of two years. Second, there were my parents. I was certain that their vision for me included college—*any* college.

An hour later, my mother scurried through the back door, fresh from her day at the museum. She had seen the envelope earlier and was curious and hopeful about the contents. She wasn't attuned to the "fat envelope, thin envelope" theory of college acceptances.

There was silence when I gave her the news. She paused to compose her thoughts while slowly looking about the room.

"What are you going to do *now*?" she finally asked.

It was important to my mother that one always have a plan.

"I dunno. I'll think of something."

"Well, you *have* to have a plan."

On rare occasions, when she felt it necessary to make her point, my mother could resort to melodrama. This was one of those times.

"If not college, the only other choice you have is the military. Those *are* your two choices, right? Have you considered the military? I can't imagine that you have. It would seem to me that you should be giving serious thought to what other colleges you may be able to get into. Make a new list. Get on with it. There are plenty of good ones right here in Boston, you know. Make the list so that you're prepared to speak with the college people at Andover when you get back. Take charge."

The military?

While trying to impress upon me the dire straits in which I found myself, her comments had had the opposite effect.

The military.

It was a simple, albeit far-fetched, solution.

I had options. Or at least *an* option.

The last person in my family who had had anything to do with the military had been discharged within months of the end of World War II. My father, like everybody else in the so-called

Greatest Generation, had been in the military. He had served in the Pentagon and then as an army lawyer in Berlin shortly after the war. He told me once that he carried a pistol. There were people in his life who still called him Colonel.

I grew up in the 1950s, when the military was still considered an honorable profession. I enjoyed war movies, particularly *To Hell and Back,* the story of Medal of Honor winner Audie Murphy. We sang "The Marines' Hymn" in kindergarten. Everybody knew the words. Dwight Eisenhower was the president of the United States. The army's officer ranks were populated with some of the most brilliant minds of the time.

A generation of young boys in search of role models needed to look no further than the American military heroes of the Second World War.

By the early 1960s, however, the glory of the enormous victories of World War II was fading. Military service was losing relevance to our mushrooming generation. It was not even faintly considered as a post–high school option for my generation of Andover boys.

The military.

I really did not want to attend college—at least not anytime soon. I was ready for a change, and here one was. And it was, after all, the law.

"No, Mom," I finally responded. "I hadn't thought of the military. Maybe I'll look into it."

Without waiting for a response, I slowly rose and headed for the desk drawer under the phone and pulled out the large Boston phone book.

Where to look?

Under A for "army" or "air force"? Let's see, navy—that's right, there's the navy. What else? The marines. Coast guard? Is the coast guard considered the military?

I have often wondered what was going through my mother's mind at that moment. What mother would want her son in the military? Certainly not mine. She had introduced the subject, in

characteristic style, to get my attention. Now that she had gotten it, what was she thinking?

I fumbled through the pages and busily wrote down the lo-
cations of the downtown recruiting offices of four branches of
the military.

I would visit them the next morning.

4

IN THE EARLY SPRING OF 1966, VIETNAM WAS STILL A country and not yet a war. I was eighteen and without a plan. But now I had an option.

The following morning, I walked down High Street to Brookline Village, crossed Route 9, and boarded the Green Line trolley to Boston.

Five minutes later the train passed through the deserted Fenway Park station. My heart began to quicken. Opening day was weeks away. If Jim Lonborg's arm held up, if Yaz could rise to the level of bygone local hero Ted Williams, this could finally be the year. It was an impossible dream to consider. The Sox were one-hundred-to-one long shots to win the American League pennant.

They were awful.

The next stop was Kenmore Square. My father's office was nearby. He was the president of Boston's prestigious Lahey Clinic Foundation. What was going through *his* mind this morning? The previous evening, he had arrived home on schedule and listened to my plans without comment or visible emotion. I suspected that on his "to do" list for today was a call to Andover to begin hatching a strategy that would get me into *some* college, somewhere. I'm sure that any thought of my actually entering military service had barely registered.

Five minutes later the trolley slowly screeched around the hard turn from the Boylston stop and lumbered into the always-busy Park Street station. The train emptied.

The United States Army recruiting office was directly across the street from the top of the subway escalator. I was in and out in less than four minutes.

"Three years," the recruiter said in response to my inquiry about enlistment terms, "unless you volunteer for the draft. Then it's two years."

I had decided by this time that I wanted to take only two years off before beginning college, for I did expect to go to college eventually. I felt that three years was too long. If I volunteered for the draft and a two-year enlistment, it could take months to be called up. That would still result in a three-year break from school.

That did it for the army.

The navy was next—four years.

The air force—four years.

Now I was becoming discouraged.

After barely fifteen minutes, the military was rapidly dwindling as an option.

My last stop was the old Custom House, which housed the recruiting office for the United States Marine Corps. The recruiter, Sergeant Miller, looked sharp in his dress blue uniform. He explained that they had a special two-year program. I could enlist now and then wait one hundred twenty days to begin active duty. There was a certain sense of urgency to his explanation; it seemed the program might not be available in June.

He suggested that I take a physical the next day, before returning to school. I would be under no obligation to actually enlist but would have the physical out of the way should I later decide to enlist. This made sense. The timing was ideal and it was only two years. I would have time to seek counsel from my parents and Andover teachers in order to make a well-informed, educated decision.

It did not occur to me to wonder why the marines were being so aggressive in their recruiting.

On March 7, 1966, two weeks prior to my visit to the United States Marine Corps recruiting office, Secretary of Defense Robert McNamara requested an authorization to have a total of 278,184 United States Marines on active duty by June 30, 1967. This was a dramatic increase over the current force level and would make the marine corps the first branch of the U.S. armed forces to have troop strength greater than its peak during the Korean War. It also explained why the marine corps just happened to have a freshly minted two-year enlistment program waiting for me.

They needed fresh bodies to meet their ballooning war quotas.

I decided to take Sergeant Miller's advice. I spent my final day of spring break walking through the surreal world of the pre-induction physical. Five of us met at the Custom House at eight A.M. and were driven to the Boston army base, the location at which all military physicals for the Boston region were administered. There were hundreds of men in their underpants wandering from one station to the next throughout the cavernous old pier. This was not the protected world of Andover. This was the real world. I felt curiously comfortable as I was herded from station to station. This surprised me. I knew my life was about to change. Even though I had not as yet enlisted, the exciting prospect of actually being a United States Marine was beginning to ferment inside of me.

Late that afternoon, as evening began to fall, the five of us were stuffed back into Sergeant Miller's automobile for the return trip to the Custom House. We'd all passed.

The sergeant first looked to the kid next to him sitting in the middle of the front seat, tousling the boy's hair with his hand as he spoke.

"Waddya say, Murphy?"

"I'm there, Sarge. When does the train leave for Parris Island?"

"Eight o'clock tonight, South Station."

"Any place I can get something to eat before I go?"

What?

My heart stopped.

I felt suddenly light-headed. I wanted to throw up. Murphy was going to Parris Island tonight? Parris Island—the notorious Marine Corps boot camp? This boy with whom I had spent the day strolling from station to station was on his way there? Tonight? What would he tell *his* mother?

Boy by boy, my new comrades fell to the solicitous Sergeant Miller. One was to go the next day, one after graduation, one after his sister's wedding. Finally Miller got to me.

"What about it, McLean?"

Four sets of eyes craned to look at me. Sergeant Miller kept his eyes forward as he navigated through the Boston rush hour traffic.

Too stunned to answer, I remained silent.

"McLean?"

Decisions, decisions. What was I to do?

Unlike five different colleges, the United States Marine Corps actually wanted me.

It was a most agreeable feeling.

The United States Marine Corps.

The eagle, globe, and anchor.

The hymn.

Tarawa.

Iwo Jima.

Me.

I had already decided not to attend college right away. There was a draft. I was healthy, and I didn't want to try to get out of it. It would be an honor to serve my country. It was the right thing to do. It was the only thing to do. Two years? I could stand on my head for two years.

I can't recall a time in my life before or since when a looming decision seemed more obvious.

I did think about Vietnam.

The prospect of war provided brief flashes of tingling excitement. I was, after all, an eighteen-year-old boy. My whole young life had been filled with endless television shows and movies of cowboys killing Indians, and Americans killing Germans and Japanese. Now it was my turn. Probably, though, my fate would be in a supply center someplace, or perhaps embassy duty. Like the recruiting posters, I would wear the distinguished Marine Corps dress blue uniform.

The prospect seemed manageable.

Vietnam would probably be over in six months, a year at most. The only war of my generation would be concluded before I had the chance to go.

Minutes later, I said, "I do," and began a clock ticking that would end one hundred twenty days later when I too would report to South Station for the long ride to Parris Island, South Carolina.

5

THE FOLLOWING DAY, TO THE STUNNED DISBELIEF OF faculty and students, I returned to school with my news.

"You did what?"

"Come on. You're kidding, right?"

"Jack, you can't be serious?"

I was eagerly looking for some reassurance, any reassurance, about my decision, especially from the faculty. I didn't expect my classmates to understand what I had done—I could barely grasp it myself—but many on the faculty were veterans. They proudly evoked their service every Memorial Day by donning their old uniforms and marching in a parade down Main Street. The headmaster was a retired colonel and a West Point graduate.

Jack Richards and Tom Lyons, both history instructors and strong supporters of me academically and personally, understood my decision. "Not an everyday thing around here, Jack, but a brave decision," they said. That was really all that I needed—some assurance that I hadn't completely lost my mind.

My graduating class comprised 251 boys. Of that number, more than fifty made the decision to attend Harvard University, twenty-five would go to Yale, twenty to Princeton, and twelve to Stanford. Matriculation to those four institutions alone represented more than 40 percent of the graduating class. The balance was evenly spread among many of the other most competitive colleges and universities in the land, including MIT, Dartmouth, the University of Pennsylvania, Amherst, Duke, and Columbia.

By the beginning of May, many seniors began to evoke an increased identity with their new institution. College T-shirts appeared. Boys who were headed to Yale began to act like Yalies—treating their Harvard- and Princeton-bound classmates with mock disdain.

"When *was* the last time your ice hockey team beat ours?" Ice hockey was king at Andover.

These dialogues did not include me.

The last big game won by my new team had been the Second World War.

There were two marines who took particular interest and pride in my pending military service. One was Fred Stott, a family friend and member of the Andover administration who had worked closely with my father on alumni matters for many years. He and his family had been especially kind to me during my five-year academic struggle at Andover. Fred had served with distinction in the Marine Corps during World War II, having been awarded the Navy Cross in Saipan. He also had been wounded and evacuated from Iwo Jima. He was quick to support my decision. No doubt he also made a consoling telephone call to my stunned father.

The other was United States Marine colonel Hank Aplington. Colonel Aplington was a distant cousin of my mother's from Derby Line, Vermont, the small town that sat across the border from her childhood home in Stanstead, Quebec. He and his family would make an annual summer day trip to our cottage there. This was the extent of my relationship with him. I had not really been aware at that time that he was in the United

States Marine Corps, although I do have a vivid memory of him standing in his bathing suit on our dock by the lake with a rock-hard body and a shaved head. Aplington was, in fact, a full colonel and, as I learned many years later, a highly decorated survivor of the World War II Pacific campaigns. He had been awarded both the Silver Star and the Bronze Star for gallantry in combat, in addition to several Purple Hearts.

He heard news of my enlistment and sent the following letter of introduction to me. In retrospect, it was an extraordinarily perceptive view into the marrow of one of America's outstanding institutions.

APO San Francisco
June 25, 1966
Letter from Col. Henry Aplington II, USMC

As of today I have been in the Marine Corps for twenty-six years. I'd like to take the occasion to welcome you to the USMC and give you my thoughts, which you may use or not as you may wish.

The men who have passed through our Corps have found it a rewarding and lasting experience. You will hear the expression, "Once a Marine, always a Marine" and it is true. As you embark on your military career, there are two things which you should keep in mind. First is that from the moment you signed your enlistment contract, you established a permanent record which can rise to plague you in the future or to which you can point as a matter of pride or reference. Second, the Corps has its fair share of no-goods who may be easy to gravitate to. Unfortunately, they and their friends usually end up in trouble. Take care to avoid them.

The great majority, however, without the advantages that you have had, are doing their darndest to improve themselves in every way. These are the ones to associate with. I have been impressed with the great number of men, some without the benefit of a high school education, who have by intelligence and hard work stood very high in the most difficult technical schools.

You will find the Corps a new experience. Military service has many features which have no counterpart in civilian life. In a way, it is like your prep school experience in that you are a part of it twenty-four hours a day. Unlike school, however, it is oriented toward the accomplishment of a mission, not toward the education of its members per se.

This leads your superiors to take a different view of you from that which your masters had and I think that it is worth reflecting on the way you will look to your superiors. They don't care who you are or where you came from. Their interest is in what sort of job you do and what sort of a Marine you are. They are engaged in a serious purpose, preparing a fighting machine, so that they are impressed by an individual only as he contributes to the functioning of that machine. They do not have the time or the interest to try to develop a man who is not interested, trying to help himself, or follow regulations. They have all the time in the world, however, to work with those who are interested in trying. A man must make or break himself.

The Marine Corps is big and proud with years of experience. It can be impersonal, but it knows what it wants. It has regulations to be followed. Many may look silly to you. Most, however, are there because they have been proven as effective ways to accomplish the mission; to fight and win wars. Things will be done the way the Marine Corps wants them done. If you do what you are told to the best of your ability, you will get along and it will be a rewarding experience. Otherwise you will get run over by the system and it won't hurt the system a bit.

You are now part of a long line of Marines who have

served their country in wars all over the world. This is a great time to come into the Corps. The Marines are doing what they exist to do here in Vietnam with pride and professionalism.

Welcome to the club.

Throughout my time in the Marine Corps, my mind would wander back to Aplington's letter. He made a key distinction between my life before the moment of my enlistment and my life beyond. Up to that point, I had been overseen by my family, friends, and Andover faculty. That would soon change. The Marine Corps cared about me as a vehicle to their own ends—winning wars. It was important, consequently, that I be well trained, well fed, well disciplined, well behaved, and that I follow orders.

The Marine Corps cared about the Marine Corps.

It was an important early lesson for this innocent child of privilege.

In early June, I learned that my fears about graduating from Andover had been warranted. I had failed trigonometry and would not graduate with my class on June 6, 1966. I still attended the graduation ceremony with my classmates, but received an empty envelope. Barby and my parents came. Though my grandparents had come up to Brookline from Elizabeth, New Jersey, my father asked that they not attend, "given the circumstances."

It was a most unhappy day.

I, however, was relieved that I actually had passed four out of my five courses—was quietly thrilled, in fact. And really, who needed trigonometry?

My American-history teacher was Tom Lyons, even then a legend at Andover. When he informed me that I had passed his rigorous course that spring with a 63 average (60 was passing), he said that I had earned every point of it. Several weeks later, I received the following letter from him:

Dear General McLean,

I know I echo the entire faculty's sentiments when I state that Andover is no prouder of any member of this class than of Private McLean. You showed a lot of people—adolescents and adults—something about character and courage in your stay here.

I wish you the best of luck in your math exam and in the months ahead, from Parris Island on. Come back and see us when you can. Our best wishes are always with you.

Sincerely,

Field Marshal Thomas von Lyons

Lyons gained a degree of national notoriety years later when candidate George W. Bush, in a rare public acknowledgment of his Andover experience, referred to Lyons in a *New York Times* article as his most outstanding teacher.

On July 2, 1966, I sat for my math makeup exam and passed with flying colors. Later that afternoon, the headmaster called me into his office and handed me my high school diploma.

Six weeks later, my father drove the short distance from Brookline to Boston's South Station to deliver me into the hands of Sergeant Miller. Miller welcomed our small group to active duty, presented us with our "official orders," and saw to it that we actually boarded the train.

Fifteen hours later, after a layover in New York and a train change in Washington, D.C., our connecting bus arrived at the United States Marine Corps Recruit Depot, Parris Island, South Carolina.

6

THE UNITED STATES MARINE CORPS RECRUIT DEPOT at Parris Island, South Carolina, occupies the entire 6,600 acres of a flat sandy Atlantic barrier island, located between Charleston, South Carolina, and Savannah, Georgia. Its mission is to train all incoming marine recruits from east of the Mississippi River. The Marine Corps described Parris Island as a place to "indoctrinate the recruit with the essential knowledge derived from almost two centuries of experience in training fighting men, and to inculcate in the individual that intangible 'esprit de corps' that is the hallmark of United States Marines."

To those of us who served, it was simply hell on earth.

Recruit training at Parris Island was tough, exhausting, and excruciatingly exacting. Its mission was to produce America's first line of defense. A Marine Corps motto was "First to Fight." This is where boys became ready, willing, and able to do so—at a moment's notice.

Historically, the spit of land was noteworthy. The first attempt to colonize South Carolina occurred with the discovery of Parris Island in 1526 by Lucas Vázquez de Ayllón, a Spaniard in search of slaves and gold. It was later briefly colonized by a group of French Huguenots who built a fort on its southeastern tip.

The first title to the island was granted in 1700. In 1715, the title passed to Alexander Parris—hence the name. Seven plantations flourished for more than 175 years until 1891, when the marines landed with a small detachment to defend a naval station there. By 1915, the island had become the recruit depot for the Marine Corps.

Over the following three years, nearly forty-one thousand recruits were trained there to man the American effort in World War I. After a postwar lull, the recruit load skyrocketed following the Japanese attack on Pearl Harbor on December 7, 1941. During the balance of that month alone, 5,272 recruits arrived. The following month the number reached 9,206. During the period 1941–1945, more than two hundred thousand marine recruits were trained on Parris Island.

Recruitment dropped at the end of World War II. When the Korean Conflict began, there were only two thousand recruits on the island. By March 1952, however, the number had ballooned again to more than twenty-four thousand. In all, more than 138,000 marines were trained during Korea.

Now Vietnam.

Our first week on Parris Island was a blur. Vázquez de Ayllón and his crew may have been ecstatic at their first sight of land viewed across the water from the east in 1526. Those of us on the charter bus crossing the causeway from the west in August 1966, however, were apprehensive at best—scared shitless at worst.

Count me among the scared shitless.

We reached Parris Island sometime after midnight and were screamed off the bus by Drill Instructor Staff Sergeant W. H. Hilton.

"If you are smoking a cigarette, you will put it out; if you are chewing gum, you will swallow it. You have thirty seconds to get off this bus, maggots, and fifteen have already passed. Move. *Move. MOVE.*"

And move we did, clambering over one another as though escaping a fire, grabbing our bags from the overhead bin and tumbling out of the bus onto the painted yellow footprints that were lined up in perfect platoon formation. There were several dazed stragglers who seconds before had been in a sound sleep. I have a vivid memory of Staff Sergeant Hilton grabbing one of them by the neck as he hit the bottom step and throwing him to the pavement.

Straggling, apparently, was not tolerated.

There had been joking on the trip down about what was in store for us—the perverse kind of banter unique to teenage boys. We all had heard stories about Parris Island; some had direct knowledge through friends or family members who had served. We were confident that we knew what was coming and were prepared to take it on. We were . . . marines.

Sort of.

In fact, we would not officially be marines until we graduated from Parris Island. Of that we were *constantly* reminded. Although we were to hold the rank of private and were to be paid accordingly ($96.50 a month), one had to learn to *be* a marine before ever being *accepted* as one within. Here, "learn" meant "earn," as I never knew before.

Once we were assembled on the footprints, Staff Sergeant Hilton asserted his authority over us as a group. We were one hundred ten boys, but by the time we graduated, we would be one.

That was made clear.

For the next several days, the only words spoken by any of us would be a resounding "YES, SIR" to any request or question that came out of Staff Sergeant Hilton's mouth. Otherwise there was silence. That evening, we were herded in loose formation through the double doors of the receiving building. Every motion was a lesson—how to open a door the Marine Corps way, how to hold it, how to move in a straight and tight line. ("Asshole to belly button, ladies. Asshole to belly button!")

Our clothes were removed, bundled, and sent home. We were given a pen and a postcard upon which to write a single line home saying that we had arrived safely. Our heads were shaved clean. Wrapped in towels, we were led to the showers to wash off the last of our "civilian scuz."

As we emerged, we passed through a gauntlet of navy corpsmen who gave us a number of shots in each arm. I had an aversion to needles and immediately, instantly abhorred corpsmen and all that was navy. That naïve opinion would change shortly after arriving in Vietnam, where I witnessed the selfless valor of the United States Navy Medical Corps. No group of individuals—marines included—ever brought greater honor to the United States Marine Corps than the navy field corpsmen.

Still wrapped in towels, we emerged from the initial processing center and walked across the parade deck to enter a cavernous supply warehouse. The now cool night air felt strangely fresh against our denuded, clean bodies. We were ordered to hold our arms out straight before us and sidestep on command. With each step, a marine would throw an additional article onto the growing bundle of military clothes that bore some resemblance to our size.

Combat boots, however, were the one exception—they were carefully fitted and issued. This was the first of two important lessons—that healthy feet and clean rifles were nonnegotiable in the Marine Corps.

Dog tags were stamped and hung around our necks, where they would remain until we were released from active duty or killed. I wear mine to this day. We were given sheets, towels, toothbrushes, soap, canteens, mess kits, razors, shaving cream, shoe polish, and all manner of necessities that would be required in our new life. We were not issued a hairbrush. Our arms, still outstretched, ached. Our heads pounded. Staff Sergeant Hilton screamed. We were neither fast enough nor good enough. We would NEVER become marines!

At the last stop we were given a seabag in which to put our new possessions. We filed outside and again fell into formation on the yellow footprints, this time more quickly and with an air of familiarity.

I had never before been in the coastal South, so the pungent early-morning low country smells mixed with military web gear that first entered my senses that morning made an indelible imprint on me, a smell I can occasionally conjure up even today.

We marched in our scratchy new outfits, seabags weighing heavily upon our shoulders, to a building across the base that would become our barracks. The stark intensity of the occasional spotlight provided the only illumination. There was no sound except the marching cadence of boots on pavement, the rustling of clothes, and the occasional clanging of a canteen. There were no more little jokes or asides among my new comrades. Staff Sergeant Hilton had by this time made vivid examples of several more boys.

We were very tired.

Home was very far away.

My platoon, number 3076, consisted of one hundred ten boys of all shapes, sizes, and colors. Andover prided itself on attracting "youth from every quarter," but the mosaic of America that was this platoon helped me understand how culturally limiting my prep school experience had been. Here, we really were from every quarter: sons of coal miners, truck drivers, farmers, convicts, factory workers, and sharecroppers from every conceivable ethnic enclave in America. There, however, the differences ended.

At any given moment of any day, we wore exactly the same clothes: white boxers and T-shirts to bed; utility pants, T-shirts, and combat boots during the day; shorts, T-shirts, and sneakers for physical training. Any self-imposed attempt at identity was stripped. We each had a footlocker at the base of our bunks in which we had exactly the same gear—down to the size and color of our toothbrushes. Noses, lips, and ears seemed disproportionate in size, given the absence of hair.

Our trips to the head were relegated to strategic moments during the day, with few exceptions. In the early morning, we were given ten minutes to shit, shower, and shave. Although there were twenty sinks, there were only eight open toilets, so the pressure to complete your business in a timely manner was extreme, as there could be as many as five or six boys in a tight line directly in front of you.

Each night, a regular fire watch schedule was established. Outfitted with a steel helmet liner—known as a chrome dome—and a web belt, each recruit would walk the squad bay in a one-hour shift, all night long. The soft cadence of boots on the concrete; the rustling of canteen, bayonet, and ammo magazine pouches; and the occasional snores were the night music of Platoon 3076.

For the next two years, guard duty became a nightly part of our lives, whether in a stateside barracks or in a Vietnam foxhole. Being awakened at three A.M. for watch relief after a physically exhausting day was one of Parris Island's greatest tortures. On the other hand, it also provided the only time to be alone with one's thoughts, which I welcomed. I needed as much time as I could find to keep my mind around what was going on.

We customarily would hit the rack at about nine-thirty P.M. The first several days, we were awakened at four-fifteen A.M. to the sound of a screaming drill instructor who, as often as not, would throw a galvanized trash can down the concrete floor of the squad bay. One hundred ten boys instantly leapt out of racks, identically clad in white boxer shorts and T-shirts. In a single motion we pulled our sheets off the bed and held them high above our heads while standing at attention in perfect rows in front of our bunks. Each set of linens was carefully examined so that bed wetters could be weeded quickly from our ranks.

There was a purpose to the madness that ensued over the next several months, and intellectually I was at peace with it. The physical and mental elements, however, were excruciating. The United States Marine Corps Recruit Depot at Parris Island, like its sister in San Diego, California, exists for three purposes: to teach group discipline, to conduct rigorous physical training, and to endow each graduate with the complete mastery of the M14 rifle. During this time we would also be taught how to be marines. This included Marine Corps history (Tun Tavern in

Philadelphia, 1775), traditions ("floor" equals "deck"), structure (chain of command), and personal hygiene (ass gets wiped
front to back). It was assumed that we knew nothing.

It wasn't long before we all felt that way.

To achieve these ends, it was necessary—critical—that each
recruit be immediately and fiercely torn down as far as he could
be taken and then slowly—ever so slowly—brought back up as
an operating unit of the larger whole. The black, white, skinny,
fat, tall, short, Okie, redneck, slum dweller, Cajun, Hoosier,
surfer were all drained. In their place, there would be *only* a perfect United States Marine. One hundred ten boys would be
molded into the same person. That person would be physically
fit, perfectly disciplined, an outstanding sharpshooter, and
trained to kill. These elements were endlessly drilled and per-
fected at Parris Island. The Marine Corps was about killing and
following orders.

Each would become second nature.

The principal vehicle for achieving group discipline was close
order drill. All of us would be required to act as one all of the
time. We'd march in formation constantly—whether going to
meals, classes, or training. We drilled on the parade deck for
hours every day, always to the unwavering command and cadence of one of our three drill instructors. Left-right-left, left-
right-left, left-right-left—endlessly—left-right-left, left-right-left.
It would be a week before we could accomplish that simplest of
tasks as a group—a week before each man in the platoon was
aware by rote of which was his right foot and which was his left.

"Your *other* right, sweetheart," was the resounding rejoinder
when one of our number had a mental lapse. Then, to be certain
that we all understood, we would be ordered to hit the deck and
do push-ups or squat thrusts until our tender hands bled and our
pampered bodies throbbed.

Left-right-left.

Left-right-left.

With that simplest of commands nearly mastered, a new one
would be introduced ("column right, HUUUH!"), then another

("to the rear, HUUUH!"), then another ("by your right flank, HUUUH!"), and always . . . *always* someone would screw up and we'd hit the deck again.

Left-right-left.

Left-right-left.

Once we began to get the hang of it, the drill instructors would lose the words and "sing" cadence in a non-English sub-language that was unique to the caller. The subtlety and inflection of each drill instructor had to be mastered—but in the end, it was all about left-right-left.

On the rare days that it was too hot to drill outside, we'd be subjected to an agonizing torture inside the barracks. While the drill instructor sang cadence, we'd kneel in formation on the concrete floor and slap our hands to the deck.

Left-right-left.

Left-right-left.

This drill was designed to toughen our hands for the rifles that would soon be added to our drilling repertoire.

Crisp loud unified noise was a requirement of close order drill. Hands had to *slap* the rifle and boots had to *slam* the pavement—every step every time. Feet and legs ached from the pounding. Soon it would be our hands. Each touch of the rifle would produce a full-force *slap*—one hundred ten slaps—in perfect unison.

Perfect.

As the hands slapped, the heels slammed.

What a mighty sound it would become.

The memory still raises the hair on my arms.

The second purpose of boot camp was physical training. By graduation, we would be in the best physical shape of our lives—better than before or after. Each day began before dawn with an hour of physical training. We'd march to the site and conduct our calisthenics in unison—push-ups, squat thrusts, and side straddle hops. After several weeks, the obstacle course was added. All of us made it or none of us made it. There was no middle ground. One of my least fond memories of physical training is of the buckets of sand that we were required to hold straight out from the sides of our bodies indeterminately.

This and countless other methods were designed to toughen us and increase discipline.

One failed, we all failed—over and over again.

Parris Island, South Carolina
August 28, 1966 (Sunday)
Letter to the McLean family

Dear home,

Things are harder and sorer than before, but my chin is still up . . . barely. There are four Drill Instructors led by SSgt. Hilton. He is crazy and impossible to please. He beats privates like flies for stupid small things. Everything we do is geared to make us killers.

Right now we're going through the PT phase—extensive physical conditioning three times a day. Above that we have one lecture a day (e.g. Marine Corps history, artificial respiration, prisoner of war situations, etc.). Tomorrow we begin drown proofing.

PT ends at the end of next week—thank God—then begins PT II which means the obstacle course, 3 mile run in full pack and helmet, and a week of bayonet practice. It is after this phase that it begins to ease up.

Love,
Jack

Before long, we began to feel ourselves come together as a cohesive unit. We began not only to drill well, but to take pride in our collective force. As a group we were becoming stronger and quicker and more obedient. Individual personalities, which were so evident during the early days, subsumed themselves to the whole. It became apparent to most of us, for the first time in our lives, that the whole was considerably stronger than the sum of its parts.

It was amazing and exhilarating.

7

"The deadliest weapon in the world is a Marine and his rifle."
—General John Pershing

IN THE COMING MONTHS WE WOULD MASTER THE RIFLE'S every nuance and provide it with unconditional love and respect. When we were ready (and only when we were ready), we would learn to fire it. To say that the relationship between a United States Marine and his rifle is sacred would be understatement in the extreme.

Early in our second week, our M14 rifles were issued. Staff Sergeant Hilton had spent much of the first weeks tearing us down individually and as a group. It was part of the deal. Consequently, he constantly pointed out that we would never be marines and that we would never learn to shoot a rifle. Based on what he'd seen, we were the single worst set of recruits to ever set foot on Parris Island. Some of the boys really began to believe it and became wildly driven and motivated. The Marine Corps had been training recruits for nearly two centuries. The Corps knew exactly what it was doing.

Eventually, Staff Sergeant Hilton was obligated to take us to the armory and at least have the weapons issued. We carefully cradled them in our arms like babies, and marched back to the barracks with our new rifles in one hand, genitals in the other, to the cadence of:

> *This is my rifle; this is my gun.*
> *This is for fightin'; this is for fun.*

By the time we got to the barracks, there was not a recruit in Platoon 3076 who would ever confuse the two terms. We were then given careful instructions on how exactly to sling the weapon to the side of the bunk. It remained there untouched for several days. Like our service numbers, the rifle serial number was committed to memory.

Several days later, we were ordered to remove the rifles from our racks and stand at attention with them by our sides. There we stood—one hundred ten of us at attention—rifles by our side, thumb and fingers positioned just so, as instructed. I double-checked, triple-checked to be certain that I looked exactly the same as everyone else, not always easy since we were permitted no head movement whatsoever while at attention. Staff Sergeant Hilton slowly began to walk down the squad bay, inspecting each recruit, moving a thumb here, adjusting a finger there. When he came before me, he stopped.

Never a good sign.

"Private McLean."

"Yes, sir."

"I can't *HEEEEEAR* you."

"YES, SIR!"

"Do you hate me?"

"NO, SIR!"

"Do you hate your rifle?"

"NO, SIR!"

"Do you think you're a fucking comedian?"

"NO, SIR!"

With that, he lunged his right hand at my neck and grasped my throat so surely and securely that all breath, indeed all movement, was rendered impossible. I was petrified.

He pushed me until I was pinned against the steel slats of my bunk. Then he pushed harder. All at once he released. As I gasped frantically for air, he unleashed a blow to my gut with the full force of his two hundred twenty pounds. I hit the deck hard. My rifle clanged to the floor and slid to the middle of the squad bay. Instantly, his hand came down again to my throat. He pulled me up and repeated the process. The third time, he hit me square in the jaw. Although I had seen it happen to others, I had no clue about what was happening or why.

"You'll NEVER be a marine, you worthless piece of shit! Get off my beautiful deck, maggot. You're getting it dirty. And for chrissakes, pick up your fuckin' rifle before I have you court-martialed!"

With that, he moved on.

I slowly stood and retrieved my rifle from the floor. I did not see any blood. As I came back to attention, I caught the eye of Tony Petrowski directly across from me. He was silently, ever so slightly, nodding toward his right side and down. Then I understood. I had been holding my rifle in my left hand, mirroring those across from me.

That afternoon I learned, in no uncertain terms, that when standing at attention with an M14 rifle, it is held firmly and securely on the right side of the body.

Nine days later, I heard my name yelled down the barracks squad bay with instructions to report to the drill instructor's office at the far end.

"Private McLean, report to the drill instructor's office immediately!"

The order was given by the recruit with the bunk closest to the office and on the drill instructor's direct command. ("Jenkins, tell McLean to get his sorry fuckin' ass down here on the double.")

This was a first for me. I had never been so called. I ran down the squad bay immediately, juggling a thousand instructions in my mind—how to stand at the door of Staff Sergeant Hilton's office (perpendicular to the right side of the opening), how to knock (swinging the left arm in a high arc over the head and slapping the top of the molding), what exactly to say ("Sir. Private McLean reporting as ordered, sir"), how to enter when instructed to do so (one step forward, right-face, two steps forward, attention, silence). The smallest slip could be disastrous.

"Sir. YES, SIR," I screamed, in a voice loud enough to peel paint off the cinder block walls.

"Oh, shut the fuck up; quit yelling at me, for chrissakes."

Stunned, I murmured, "Sir. Yes, sir."

"What *do* you put in those letters home that you write?" Hilton quietly asked in a manner that was more rhetorical than quizzical. "I knew I should have been keeping a closer eye on you."

Letters home?

My mind raced.

What could I have said in a letter that might have gotten back here somehow? Surely nothing that I wrote to my parents. Although I endeavored to be forthright, I did try to protect them from some of the more graphic horrors of Parris Island, particularly the physical abuse under Staff Sergeant Hilton that was a fact of our everyday life. I didn't necessarily feel that way when writing others, though, and may have mentioned the rifle incident to someone, but I was at a loss to recall.

So I didn't answer.

We were often told that what went on inside the barracks of Platoon 3076 stayed inside the barracks of Platoon 3076. When we wrote home, we were to speak only of how good the food was or how magnificently our boots were shined. Occasionally we would be drilled on this. After a particularly severe beating of a hapless recruit, Staff Sergeant Hilton might look around and ask, "Any of you fuck heads see that?" We would all shake our heads. The message was clear.

We were not to discuss physical abuse by drill instructors outside of the barracks.

"Colonel Jameson wants to see you. You know who he is?"

Colonel Jameson?

Familiar.

Let me think.

Colonel Jameson was a name in the chain of command.

That's right.

The chain of command.

We had had to memorize the chain of command during our first week. I think he was three people above Staff Sergeant Hilton and four people down from the president of the United States.

"Yes, sir." But please don't ask me what his job is.

"Well, he wants to see you and he wants to see you right now. His office is over there on the other side of the parade deck." With that, Staff Sergeant Hilton pointed out the window of his small office in the direction of a building I recognized as the location of our classrooms. "March over there. Go in that front door. They are waiting for you. I'll be right here when you get back. Right here."

"Aye, aye, sir."

"Private McLean?"

"Sir. Yes, sir." Loud enough for him to hear, not loud enough to piss him off.

"You ever tell anybody what goes on in here in one of those fancy letters you write?"

"Sir. No, sir!"

"Good. You don't plan on starting now, do you?"

"Sir. No, sir."

"What goes on inside the barracks of Platoon 3076 stays inside the barracks of Platoon 3076. You know that, right?"

"Sir. Yes, sir."

"You better not fuck this up, you know what I mean? You may never get off this little island. Do you understand me, Private McLean?" Not exactly threatening, maybe even a little nervous.

"Sir. Yes, sir."

What was going on?

My mind raced through all the possibilities as I marched, alone, across the parade deck to the battalion headquarters. They were the first steps that I had taken outside of platoon formation in a month. I could feel Staff Sergeant Hilton's eyes hard on my back.

I arrived at the building, pulled open the door, and was at once directed into a large office on the left. The walls were covered with old photographs, plaques, and a color portrait of Lyndon Baines Johnson, the thirty-sixth president of the United States, and the first name in my chain of command. Four officers faced me. The one with the most ribbons made introductions. They were the first officers I saw at Parris Island, and thereby in the Marine Corps as well. I knew that they were officers because they had markings on their collars instead of their sleeves. We weren't far enough along in our training, however, for me to know what kind of officers they were.

"Good morning, Private. Please be seated." The officer speaking was a colonel. I knew that because he had a little bird on his collar. Colonels and generals were easy to spot.

Birds and stars.

"Sir. Aye, aye, sir." I sat. Others followed.

The chairs were loosely arranged in a semicircle with all eyes on me.

"Private," the colonel continued, "how are you liking things here on Parris Island?"

I tried to remember all that Staff Sergeant Hilton had taught us about speaking with officers. I now wished I'd paid more attention. I did remember that we weren't supposed to look them in the eye, but always just a few inches off to the side. This was counter to everything I had ever learned growing up, but I focused hard on the colonel's right ear. We also were never to speak in the first person. I was trying hard to sit at attention. We hadn't learned how to do that.

If Hilton could strangle us for the slightest infraction, what could a colonel do?

"Sir, the private likes Parris Island, sir."

"We know the training can be rough sometimes, Private. Do you think the training is rough?"

What was the right answer? I had a fifty-fifty shot.

"Sir. Yes, sir."

Stay focused on the ear, Jack.

"How do you like your drill instructors, Private?"

Huh? Was he kidding?

No, he appeared serious, but I knew better than to speak the truth.

Again, what was the right answer?

"Sir, the private likes his drill instructors okay, sir."

"They can be pretty tough sometimes, though, can't they?"

I was now becoming uncomfortable about the direction of the questions.

I slowly nodded silently.

"Private McLean, I'm going to ask you an important question and it is important that you give me a truthful answer. Do you understand me, son?"

"Sir. Yes, sir," I replied, barely above a whisper.

"Private McLean, have you ever been struck by a drill instructor during your time here at Parris Island?"

Shit.

"Sir, the private doesn't understand the question, sir."

What a stupid response. I understood the question perfectly, but I needed time to gather myself.

"Fairly simple question, Private. Have you ever been hit by a drill instructor? You know, hit, like with a fist?"

No matter what happened here, these officers would be gone from my life shortly. I would, however, still have to sleep with Staff Sergeant Hilton.

So I lied.

"Sir. No, sir."

"No? Again, Private, it's important that you tell us the truth. We're not going to let anything bad happen to you. Please tell me the truth now. Have you ever been hit by a drill instructor or seen anyone else in the platoon hit by a drill instructor?"

All eyes were focused on me.

"Sir. No, sir."

Now I was living the lie. It was getting easier.

"Okay. I believe you, son. Now, have you ever written a letter home telling anyone that you've ever been beaten?"

Let's see. Think. I told one or two friends. I may have written something to Mr. Richards, one of my teachers at Andover. I couldn't think of anyone else. Did they read your mail here? How could I have been so stupid?

"Sir. No, sir."

"Private McLean, does the name Jack Richards mean anything to you?"

Fuck. I'm fucked.

"Private?"

The air had escaped from my lungs. All blood had left my face. I had to sit. I was sitting. I had to lie down. I felt shame. I was cornered. Caught. I remembered the letter now. I had told him about the rifle incident with Staff Sergeant Hilton in great detail. He must have said something to somebody. Good intentions, perhaps, since Parris Island was not that many years removed from the infamous night when an out-of-control drill instructor had marched several in his platoon to their death in the surrounding swamps.

They had the letter; there was no way out.

"Sir. Yes, sir."

"And did you write a letter telling him that you'd been hit by a drill instructor here on Parris Island?"

"Sir. Yes, sir."

"So Private McLean, either you lied in the letter or you are lying to us. Which is it, son?"

No right answer either way, but I still had six more weeks with Platoon 3076.

"The letter, sir."

The inquisition was over in another ten minutes, during which time it was made clear that I was in fact a liar and that there was no place in the United States Marine Corps for dishonesty.

Did I understand?

Did I really understand?

I was told to immediately write a letter to Richards acknowledging that I had lied so that he could then inform the individual who had issued the complaint, thereby exonerating the United States Marine Corps of any culpability in this unfortunate episode.

As I marched back across the parade deck, it occurred to me that there probably wasn't an officer in that room who had actually believed that I had not been hit, but I felt deep shame for my participation in the entire incident nonetheless.

Staff Sergeant Hilton was waiting as I reentered the barracks.

Who was in the room?

What did they have on their collars?

What did they ask?

What did you say?

Are you sure?

Tell me again.

After an exhaustive recounting, a very relieved Staff Sergeant Hilton ordered me back to my rack area to join the others in the daily domestic rituals of rifle cleaning and shoe spit-shining. I was frightened and relieved beyond all imagination. Any hope that I had had of remaining anonymous at Parris Island disappeared that day.

Not coincidentally, so did any chance that Staff Sergeant Hilton, or any other drill instructor, would ever touch me again.

"The Marine Corps Builds Men."

For a generation, that powerful slogan attracted young boys like me to the United States Marine Corps. We all were eager to look like the mighty marine on the recruiting poster in the dress blue uniform, of whom family, community, and country would be proud. The marines were masters at the exterior part—twelve weeks of boot camp turned out an admirable physical specimen indeed. But the true measure of a man lies within. Colonel Aplington, in his letter to me months before, had said that "a man must make or break himself." Which had I done? I wasn't certain. The letter had been the truth. I'm certain that all involved knew that. My subsequent lies about it were shameful. It would be decades before I was able to reconcile the two.

8

DURING THE LAST WEEK OF SEPTEMBER, WE CAREFULLY folded and stowed all of our gear into seabags that were loaded onto a waiting truck. Equipped with our rifles and field marching packs, we fell into formation and with a resounding "Platoon 3076, FO'ARD HUUUH," bid farewell to the 3rd Battalion area for the first time, and headed, double-time, several miles to the rifle range. I was excited. Certainly the toughest part of boot camp was over. Now would come the serious and sober business of the rifle.

As we left the area, the envious eyes of the newer recruits focused on us as we marched past the parade deck, obstacle course, and physical training fields. We were on our way to the range. We stood tall. We were proud. We were becoming marines. The drill instructor sang what would be our unending cadence for the next two weeks:

We don't want no Maggie's drawers.
All we want is fives and fours.
Left-right-left.
Left-right-left . . .

Fives and fours were the highest scores for each target. Maggie's drawers, on the other hand, represented a total miss of the target. On such occasions, the spotter would wave a red flag on a long stick from beneath the target bunker.

As it turned out, I was completely wrong about the rifle range. The new tone set upon arrival was all too familiar. We moved into the barracks, removed our gear from the seabags, stowed it in footlockers, and were immediately informed by Staff Sergeant Hilton that we had five minutes to prepare for a "junk on the bunk" inspection. This hideous drill involved laying all of our gear on the bunk in a perfectly predetermined order with no margin for error.

Each bunk would be identically laid out, as we had exactly the same gear—not a toothbrush more, not a pair of socks less. The slightest wrinkle on a uniform, the tiniest flaw on a spit-shined shoe, the smallest corner of unpolished brass, were all cause for unimagined castigation. One flaw with one person's gear, and we all would suffer. That was the way it worked.

It was, of course, a setup.

One hundred ten mostly teenage boys had been given five minutes to take everything they owned from a footlocker, stuff it into a seabag, and throw it onto a truck. At the other end, we'd been given five minutes to find our seabag, unload it into a footlocker, make up the new bunk, and then, upon it, display perfectly all that we owned. Someone would be missing a facecloth or a shoelace. Someone, God forbid, would have a piece of contraband—perhaps a stick of chewing gum sent by a girlfriend, or a cigarette, or a small box of cereal purloined from the mess hall.

Staff Sergeant Hilton slowly strutted down the squad bay, uniform perfectly creased, beady eyes perfectly focused, Smokey the Bear hat perfectly tipped forward.

We were fucked.

He randomly stopped in front of Private Darnell's bunk. Nothing. Then Garcia's. Nothing. He turned toward me, and my heart leapt into my throat. He walked over and saw something on the bunk next to mine. I have no recollection what it might have been, but Staff Sergeant Hilton went nuts. He tipped the entire bunk over, threw the mattress out the open second-floor window, and then picked up the footlocker and threw it down the squad bay. He mirrored the same exercise with three other displays before he began to regain his composure. His final insult was to empty several cans of talcum powder over all in sight.

"This place looks like a shit hole, you maggots."

He was pissed.

"Get this dump squared away. Sanchez, you'd better get that fuckin' mattress back up here before the captain sees it or you'll really be in a world of shit."

So began our fortnight at the rifle range.

The following morning we had PT and drilled just as though we were back at battalion. We then attended our first class—we called it Snapping-In 101. Before we could shoot the rifle, we had to learn how to hold the rifle. Preparation was everything. This preparation was called snapping-in. We began with the standing position. We'd stand at the ready, create a hasty sling around the left arm, and spread our feet to a comfortable distance apart. We'd then place the rifle against the right shoulder, with the left arm under the rifle supporting it in the most balanced position. Finally, we'd grip the stock with the right hand while holding the right elbow in line with or above the shoulder. Above all, it was important to keep the body erect. To be certain that we understood this, we were ordered to hold the position without moving a hair for one hour.

We could then take a sip of water, and repeat the process.

The following days brought more new positions to be mastered. First was the sitting position, which included a new set of contortions that bore little resemblance to those of the day before, other than the pain involved. The closer to the ground, the steadier the shot. Every few minutes, the drill instructor's right

foot would bear down on your back to be certain you understood what "closer to the ground" meant. Don't move a hair for
one hour.

Take a sip of water.

Repeat.

The kneeling position was mastered on day three and the
prone position on day four. On days five and six we snapped-in,
drilled, did PT, and attended classes that taught us what to expect the following week when the actual shooting began.

At the beginning of the second week, we went to the shooting range for the first time. After hours of sight adjustment,
we snapped-in at the one-hundred-yard line and fired several
rounds of live ammunition. With each early awkward round
fired, an instructor would lean down and whisper our new
mantra into our ringing ears, "Breathe, relax, aim, slack, and
squeeze, motherfucker." He might then continue for emphasis,
"You better hit that target, shit head, or you are *never* getting off
this island."

Qualification, two days later, was all business. We woke up
early, skipped PT and drilling, had a light breakfast, and were on
the range by six A.M. There were smoking smudge pots along the
firing line. We each carefully applied the soot to the top of our
cheeks so that our sweat would not reflect the sun back into our
eyes. We then awaited our turn to shoot at the targets. At two
hundred yards, we were to fire from the standing and kneeling
positions. At three hundred yards, we'd use the kneeling and sitting positions. At five hundred yards, we'd fire from the prone
position.

By the end of the day, all but two of us had qualified. We
were mostly satisfied and enormously relieved. The two non-
qualifiers did not go directly to hell, as Staff Sergeant Hilton had
promised, but they were quietly removed from Platoon 3076
and placed in a special platoon to become "motivated."

Our mastery of the rifle complete, we proudly made the

return march to the 3rd Battalion area. The endless new facts and skills that we had mastered over the previous two weeks brought a smile to my face as I recalled my Andover roommate Spike Tolman. Spike was so knowledgeable about early rock and roll music that he could, when prompted with only the *time* of a song on the B side of a 45 rpm record, instantly come up with the title of the A-side hit.

"Spike, two minutes, fifty-two seconds?"

" 'Great Balls of Fire.' Jerry Lee Lewis. Sun Records," he would reply without so much as drawing a breath. Two minutes, fifty-two seconds was the time of the little known (except to Spike) flip side titled, appropriately, "You Win Again." Spike could do this over and over through dozens of records until the asker became bored.

So it became with a United States Marine and his M14 rifle. There are facts about the M14 rifle that most marines will remember long after they've forgotten their own names—such was the rigor of Marine Corps rifle training.

"PRIVATE McLEAN."

"SIR. YES, SIR."

"11.09."

"SIR. The weight of my 7.62 mm gas operated, magazine fed, air cooled shoulder weapon, with sling, with magazine, with cleaning gear, and with twenty rounds of NATO 7.62 caliber ammo. SIR."

The only unknown element that had existed when we'd arrived on the range had to do not with the weapon but with the marine who fired it. It did not remain that way for long.

Several years ago, a sniper terrorized the greater Washington, D.C., area for months. News outlets speculated that the shooter might be a highly trained ex-military sniper and, thereby, simple to locate. In fact, any marine who ever graduated from boot camp is capable of hitting and killing a human target at five hundred yards *without* a telescopic scope. Every time.

That's five football fields.

It never leaves you.

....

On the afternoon prior to our graduation, Staff Sergeant Hilton
gathered us in the barracks for a chilling peek at the reality that
would exist for us outside the isolated confines of Parris Island.
As we rustled into place around him, he held the orders for our
permanent assignments over his head for us all to see. There was
an MOS (Military Occupation Specialty) number and duty location for each of the remaining one hundred eight members of
Platoon 3076. He began, as he always did, at the beginning of
the alphabet with Private Thomas Jefferson Agbisit.

"AGBISIT." Long pause. "0311, WESTPAC. Well, shit-for-
brains, looks like the commandant wants you to go kill some
fuckin' gooks! OUTSTANDING."

The names continued.

"ANDERSON." Long pause. "0311, WESTPAC."

"BERRINGTON." Long pause. "0311, WESTPAC."

"You lucky shits, you're going to go see some ACTION. I
hope like hell you worthless fucks paid attention here."

After several names, there emerged a chilling recognition of
the ultimate purpose for which we had been trained. Most of
Platoon 3076 was going to war. The numbers 03 meant infantry.
The 11 indicated a rifleman. WESTPAC was short for Western
Pacific. For nearly all, that meant Vietnam. By the time he
reached the L's, my nostrils began to clear, and my senses height-
ened. I felt dizzy. Obviously the situation in Vietnam had
changed dramatically during the brief period that we had been
isolated in boot camp.

"McLEAN." Long pause. "3042." Long pause. "SUPPLY
SCHOOL." Long pause. "CAMP LEJEUNE."

Huh? I was not sure what I had heard, but I did know what
I had *not* heard. The number 30 meant supply, and the 42, I later
found out, was a subset that meant mechanized. Mechanized
supply.

"McLEAN—you DUMB motherfucker, you IGNORANT
son of a bitch, you USELESS piece of shit, you . . . you . . . you

... MAGGOT." Staff Sergeant Hilton enjoyed editorializing about each marine's new assignment. "Those assholes up in Washington have decided to teach you computers—whatever the fuck they are! Sounds like you're not GOOD enough to go kill those little gook bastards."

Then, no kidding, he actually *smiled*.

One minute earlier, I had been frightened.

Vietnam.

War.

Now I was disappointed. The United States Marine Corps was about war. There was a war going on, and most of my platoon mates were shipping out. But I wasn't. It was a most disorienting feeling. I had difficulty identifying its source.

Supply school?

What a waste of all I'd been through.

There never was a time, from the moment of my enlistment, when I had actually given serious thought to going to Vietnam. I had pondered the idea, certainly, and had had many "what if" discussions with family and friends, but I had assumed that, were I to go, the choice would be mine. Years later, friends would ask how I could have been so naïve, and perhaps they were right.

Now I wanted to go. And, supply school or not, eventually I would be going. We would all be going. The war was escalating rapidly. Most of my platoon had just been assigned to combat units and would be in Vietnam in a matter of weeks. Every one of us and thousands more would be needed to feed the burgeoning war. I knew that I had just dodged a bullet, yet deep down, below my unease, I knew that I had been given only a reprieve, for soon I too would be going to Vietnam to fight side by side with my Parris Island brothers. I felt a bubbling tingle of excitement, fear, and pride knowing that I would serve.

Really serve.

But yes.

Supply school first.

Graduation was the proudest day of my life. Mom, Dad, and Barby came down from Boston, and were rendered nearly speechless by the whole scene. Nothing in their lives or experience could possibly have prepared them for this. Throughout Parris Island, thousands of identically clad boys, of all backgrounds, heights, and colors were marching in unison, now components of tightly disciplined units. There was the omnipresent cadence of boots on pavement and hands on rifles. The platoons moved forward and then sideways and then to the rear while moving their weapons from one shoulder to the other. The precision was mesmerizing.

My mother loved the poetic swagger of the drill instructors, and was most admiring as she'd watched the drilling recruit platoons pass by. She particularly enjoyed the singing cadence. The drill instructor would sing out a line to the cadence, each beat synchronized with the left-right-left of the boots striking the parade deck. We would then respond in unison:

One Marine Corps color is gold—
Shows the world—we are bold.
Left-right-left.
Left-right-left.

Mother was less enamored with the next cadence that she heard:

Another Marine Corps color is red—
Rep-re-sents the blood we shed.
Left-right-left.
Left-right-left.

She turned and silently walked off by herself as the final cadence assaulted her ears:

If I die in a combat zone,
Box me up and send me home.

Wrap my arms around my chest.
Tell the world I done my best.
Left-right-left.
Left-right-left.

The Marine Corps expected us, on this our graduation day, to have perfect group discipline, to be in top physical shape, and to have complete mastery of the M14 rifle. We were there on all counts. Several days before, Platoon 3076 had won the series S drill competition—the highest prize for a recruit platoon. Staff Sergeant Hilton had been ecstatic.

It had been his goal from our first day.

He was proud of us.

It's hard to imagine that we could have stood taller or moved with crisper precision than we did that morning. With our parents in the stands and Staff Sergeant Hilton singing the cadence, there could be no group of individuals on the planet that could hold a candle to the one hundred eight boys of Platoon 3076.

We sang cadence in response to his lead as we marched across the island to the waiting ceremonial parade:

One, two, three, four.
United—States—Marine—Corps.
This is—what we—asked—for.
Three—thousand—seventy—six.
We're the—best.
Of all the—rest.
Left-right-left.
Left-right-left.

The three platoons of our graduating series marched in perfect formation across the main parade deck in front of a grandstand that had been erected for the occasion. As we turned "eyes right" to the reviewing stand, the band played "The Marines' Hymn." A sense of accomplishment and purpose washed over me. I had learned my lessons well and, together with my comrades, had *earned* the title of United States Marine.

Several minutes later, we heard our final words as recruits: "Platoon . . . three . . . thousand . . . seventy . . . six . . . DIIIIISSSS-MISSED."

It was official.

I was now a private in the United States Marine Corps.

The lessons of Parris Island were incalculable, and I have no doubt that they saved my life time and again while I was under enemy fire in Vietnam. Each marine, whether eventually a cook or a pilot, is first trained to be a combat infantryman. He must be a highly trained rifleman, and requalify as such every year. He must be in top physical shape and stay that way throughout his tour. He must respect his equipment. Each marine knows that, no matter his duty assignment, he must be prepared to go into combat in an infantry rifle squad anywhere in the world on a moment's notice. He must obey orders without hesitation, and execute his assigned duties without question.

From the first night on the yellow footprints, we learned that, as marines, we were in it together. If one fell behind, we pulled him forward with the rest of us. His success was our success. We respected one another. "Gung Ho" is a Marine Corps motto. It is derived from the Chinese and means "working together." The other more familiar Marine Corps motto is "Semper Fidelis," which is Latin for "always faithful." We worked together and were always faithful. These were the lessons of Parris Island.

We reveled in the observation by First Lady Eleanor Roosevelt twenty-five years before,

> The marines I have seen around the world have the cleanest bodies, the filthiest minds, the highest morale, and the lowest morals of any group of animals I have ever seen. Thank God for the United States Marine Corps!

One year after my graduation from Parris Island, I was in Vietnam, fighting side by side with my marine brothers, when I was shot at with live ammo for the first time. During the ensuing battle and the others that followed, I was confused, disoriented, and scared to death—every time—but I was never alone. There was always another marine nearby. He also was confused, disoriented, scared to death—but he had *me* nearby. That was the way it worked in the Marine Corps. Together we'd figure something out. As long as there was another marine, we were a unit. It was taught from the moment that we arrived on Parris Island. It continues to exist in me and the others to this day. There is no challenge too great, no night so dark that the presence of another marine—past or present—fails to give me the courage and faith that together we are capable of anything.

Camp Geiger is part of Camp Lejeune, the sprawling Marine Corps base located on the North Carolina coast near the town of Jacksonville. All marine recruits east of the Mississippi who have completed their basic training at Parris Island go there directly by bus the morning after graduation to complete a six-week infantry training course. Those in the West attend boot camp in San Diego and infantry training at Camp Pendleton, Lejeune's enormous counterpart on the Southern California coast.

At Parris Island we drilled, shot, and exercised by rote. The only way was the Marine Corps way. At Camp Geiger, we became creative. We were taught to think like marines by mastering the principles of infantry combat as well as squad and platoon tactics. We were trained on every individual and crew-served weapon in the Marine Corps arsenal, and were presented with situations for their use. The mission was to convert us from disciplined boot camp graduates into self-confident and thinking marines capable of immediately joining a combat-ready infantry fire team.

For many of us, that moment was now short weeks away.

The strain caused by the continuing buildup in Vietnam was apparent everywhere. New brick barracks were under construction to augment the tent cities that were popping up. There were sporadic shortages of rifles, uniforms, and general military supplies. An escalating urgency permeated our every activity. Drills that used to begin with "*If* this happens . . ." had changed to "*When* this happens . . ."

Actual combat was now a certainty for every one of us.

For the first time, several of our instructors were Vietnam veterans. To them, our education was not theory—it was real. They had been shot at. They had seen people get killed. They had been wounded.

All knew the value of training and how critical it would become when we ourselves were under fire.

9

I COMPLETED MY INFANTRY TRAINING ON NOVEMBER
10, 1966, the 191st birthday of the United States Marine Corps,
and returned home to Brookline for three weeks of leave. My
homecoming was disorienting. Civilian life seemed chaotic and
unstructured. I felt naked without the rifle that had been with
me since the second week of boot camp. I wasn't sure what to do
with my new body. I was twenty pounds heavier than when I'd
left. None of my old clothes fit.

I wondered at my muscled strength. My shoulders were
broad, my thighs were like granite, and my general appearance
was, well, mean. My every stance was awkward. Making sen-
tences out of words became a thoughtful struggle. As my mother
noted, it was palpable the degree to which things had changed in
my life during those long weeks at Parris Island, while little at
home seemed to have changed at all.

After the initial euphoria, which included my first private
visit to a bathroom in more than three months, I began to feel
uncomfortable. Back under my parents' roof, I settled into old
routines that made me feel more like a boy than the man I was
becoming. Dad went to work, Barb went to school, and Mom

went about her daily life. I was bored. I actually missed the structured daily regimen of boot camp.

Several days after my arrival home, I took a bus up to Hanover, New Hampshire, to surprise my Andover friend Lou Maranzana with a visit. He was a freshman at Dartmouth College. As night fell, I trudged up three flights of stairs, found his room, and entered. I slowly looked around, and the sight was an assault on my barracks-trained sensibilities. Books and magazines were strewn about the dormitory room floor, intermingled with empty beer and soda cans, and food wrappers. One glaring overhead bulb brought the only illumination. As I absorbed the scene, I cringed at the thought of how Staff Sergeant Hilton might have reacted to such chaos.

I was, in fact, cringing at the chaos myself.

Lou was reclined on a threadbare sofa reading a book. Our eyes caught as the door opened fully. We were speechless. Something was very different. Had I changed, or had Lou? He looked the same to me, but his expression told me that the feeling was not mutual. He rose slowly and exhaled loudly while taking me in. I was twenty pounds heavier, shaved bald, and in perfect physical shape. As many friends and family members told me during those weeks, I was a formidable sight to behold. Lou broke into a broad smile, muttered a disbelieving "holy shit" under his breath, and we hugged.

He found me a beer while I lit a cigarette and flopped onto the corner of the sofa. It was a difficult moment. It was hard to know where to begin. The books on the floor related to subjects as diverse as Einstein and romantic poetry. I was more aware of what I did not see than what I did see, however. There was no footlocker, no rifle, no spit-shined boots, and, well, no control.

Lou, like most people that I encountered during boot leave, wanted to know everything about where I had been and what I had experienced. Like Lou, however, most people had no place to put the information. To them, I was devoid of context. I was, after all, the only person among my family and friends who had become a United States Marine. There was an enormous disconnect. I asked Lou about college, his courses, girls, and the Ivy League football he played. "It's college," he said dismissively. "Just college, Jack, that's all." With the wave of a hand, he outlined the panorama of the room. There was nothing to it.

His life could be explained to me with the wave of a hand.

My life, however, had become complex. I could find few words to describe it. The previous March, word of my enlistment had made me a curiosity among my Andover classmates. Now I was a marine, and they were college freshmen. The chasm had become deep and institutionalized. We were increasingly very different. Although everyone I knew from my previous life was like them, they knew no one like me.

Not even one person.

For an entire generation of college boys, the thought of joining the military was beyond remote. The college draft deferment ensured that the ignorance would continue for another four years. My closest friends occasionally tried to appreciate my experience and to understand my rapidly changing life, but for the most part, they had no place to process the information—my experience was that remote to them. I was regarded as an oddity.

The balance of my leave sped by, and I felt increasingly disconnected. The Marine Corps, to which I'd be returning shortly, was putting me in the backwater of supply. I was about to go from the central focus of war preparation to the exiled purgatory of supply school, followed by a remote duty station. Vietnam was now where the action was for the Marine Corps. It was all that I had been trained for. Most of my former platoon mates were on their way. In both my personal life and my new professional life, I was rapidly flowing out of the mainstream.

As my leave came to a close, I joined my family on our annual trek to Elizabeth, New Jersey, to celebrate the Thanksgiving holiday with my father's parents. It too was awkward. Cousins and other family members were locked into traditional roles of prep schools, college, and first jobs. My grandmother, with so much family to be proud of, was dazed and confused when it came to me. For the first time in her life, she was confronted with the real possibility that by next Thanksgiving a member of her family would be absent and in harm's way half a world away.

My grandfather alone stood tall that day in my mind's eye. He understood what I was doing and was immensely proud of the decision that I had made. Our freedom was a fragile institution, and, given his life experience, he well appreciated the need to defend it at every turn. Grandpa was a bourbon-drinking, cigar-smoking former six-term Republican congressman from New Jersey's sixth district. His childhood years had been spent as a page in the United States Senate. His twelve years in Congress exactly overlaid the first three terms of President Franklin Delano Roosevelt.

Grandpa had provided me with many of my most lasting childhood memories. He took me to my first baseball game in 1954 to see a remarkable young phenom named Willie Mays at the Polo Grounds in New York City. He later introduced me to the Metropolitan Museum of Art in New York to see the newly acquired Rembrandt masterpiece *Aristotle Contemplating the Bust of Homer*.

My grandfather's first association with war came one April afternoon in 1898 when, as a twelve-year-old Senate telephone operator, he answered the call from President William McKinley requesting a congressional war declaration against Spain.

Nineteen years later, while a young lawyer, he watched as the United States sent forces to Europe to execute the final push that ended World War I. On December 8, 1941, the day after the Japanese attack on Pearl Harbor, as a fifth-term congressman, he cast a vote to declare war on Japan. In 1950, while he was serving as a judge in Union County, New Jersey, the United States entered into the war in Korea.

Grandpa knew that our freedoms were to be cherished and defended. Sometimes, as with World War II, the enemies were clear and present. Other times, as with Spain and Korea, the issues were less obvious. As a patriotic American, however,

Grandpa had long understood that national service on any level was both a privilege and, on occasion, a necessity.

On this Thanksgiving Day, he quietly pulled me aside after dinner and expressed his appreciation for my decision to enlist in the United States Marine Corps, and expressed his deep pride that I would be serving the United States during a time of national need.

10

ON NOVEMBER 29, 1966, I TRAVELED BACK TO CAMP Lejeune and began a course in mechanized supply at the Marine Corps Supply School at Mountfort Point. A select group of us had been chosen out of boot camp to learn a new computerized supply system that was being implemented by the Marine Corps. It was as safe an assignment as existed in the marines at that time.

Our days were spent in classes learning how to type and do basic accounting and property requisitioning. There was little discipline or physical training during our six-week course. The war seemed a world away. Each day further separated us from the airtight discipline of Parris Island and the travails of our former platoon mates, now en route to Vietnam. With our new training, we were all destined to be stationed at one of the two huge stateside United States Marine Corps supply centers, in Albany, Georgia, and Barstow, California.

Graduation was held on February 3, 1967. Given the choice of the two available duty stations, I chose Barstow, California. It was 1967. California was sun, the Beach Boys, hot cars, fast food, and beautiful girls. It was an appealing image to a nineteen-year-old boy.

I could not deny, however, an unscratchable itch to go to Vietnam, to fulfill that to which all of my training had pointed. I wanted to be a part of it. I wanted to go. I wasn't what would later become known as a hawk. I had yet to form any political thought about the right or wrong of American involvement in Vietnam. I was nineteen years old, and, despite my Barstow duty station, I knew that it was still possible that I might go to war with the United States Marine Corps.

How cool was that?

Such was the thinking of this teenage boy. To this day, it's a continuing marvel to me that any boy, during any period in world history, has ever reached his twenty-first birthday.

The United States Marine Corps supply center in Barstow sprawled over wide stretches of the Mojave Desert. Outside, all manner of military apparatus, including tanks, artillery, and Jeeps, were lined up for miles. Inside the dozen enormous warehouses lay the clothes, web gear, and ordnance to outfit the exploding marine population in Vietnam. That was what we did in Barstow.

Military life there was civilized. A large contingent of my supply school classmates accompanied me, including Sid MacLeod, my closest friend and constant companion. We'd been inseparable since Camp Geiger. Sid hailed from McLean, Virginia, which we saw as a curious coincidence. He had attended a year of college but had yearned for something else. Like me, with little warning to his parents, he had quietly enlisted in the United States Marine Corps.

Every payday we'd head to the slop chute for a beer. Sid would put the Beach Boys classic "God Only Knows" on the jukebox. We'd order another round and wonder what might become of our lives.

I was nineteen. Sid was twenty.

We each had fifteen months left in the Marine Corps. Sid wanted to go to Vietnam. I wanted to go as well, but not enough to actually raise my hand—not that it would have mattered. Sid had been volunteering fruitlessly for ten months.

He was six feet tall with bright blond hair worn in a buzz cut. If you were looking for a marine out of central casting, it would have been Sid. Then again, if you were looking for a more unlikely candidate than me to be in the marines, it would have been Sid. He was intelligent, sensitive, funny as hell, controlled, patient, and intolerant of chickenshit.

A year later Sid was dead, killed in action in Khe Sanh. I was a few miles away, celebrating my twenty-first birthday on the DMZ, a brief week before our unit was overrun by a regiment of the North Vietnamese Army.

On a Sunday evening sixteen years later, my eight-year-old daughter, Sarah, handed me a folded piece of yellow-lined paper. She and her mother had just returned from a trip to Washington to visit friends and had taken time to visit the newly dedicated Vietnam Veterans Memorial. I unfolded the paper to find a pencil rubbing of the name Sidney M. MacLeod. It was visible evidence of the fact that Sid was dead and not just in deep hiding like all of my other Marine Corps buddies.

In Barstow, Sid and I lived in a small air-conditioned Quonset hut with forty other guys and worked with civilians in eight-hour shifts in the office of a warehouse. Because of the increasing activity overseas, all of the supply warehouses were operating twenty-four hours a day. There was a minimum of petty harassment. We did have a brief formation every morning, sounded off, and maybe did a few squat thrusts and side straddle hops. Rifles were issued and cleaned every day—a constant reminder that we were still, in fact, in the United States Marine Corps. Off time during the day, though, was spent baking at the base pool. Evenings were spent reading, writing letters, or playing endless games of casino and hearts. Once or twice a week we would venture out to drink beer. Once a month we'd take the long bus ride to Las Vegas or L.A., spend our monthly pay of $96.50, and return to base happily broke until the next payday.

It was deathly boring.

All around us, there was evidence of the military buildup that was taking place in Vietnam. The volume of the material that we processed in and out of Barstow every day mounted. In boot camp it had been a rarity to see a marine who had actually been in a war. Now, barely five months later, a constant stream of hardened veterans had begun to trickle back from Vietnam.

The stream became a torrent by summer.

As the days grew longer, the desert heat grew more oppressive. The news from back East was of record snow and cold, and the Boston Strangler, who held the region in a horrifying grip of terror. The news from the opposite direction was all Vietnam—escalating troop deployments and skyrocketing casualties. It was beginning to become, as author David Halberstam described in his dispatches from the front, a "quagmire."

In early March, I accepted the invitation of a barracks mate to spend a weekend with his family in Bakersfield. It was an incredible thirty-six hours that was like no weekend home from Andover ever was. This was the first time I had visited the home of a fellow marine and gotten a glimpse into his other life. No question, we came from different places. Several times over the following days, the words from Hank Aplington's letter after my enlistment rang in my ears.

> The Corps has its fair share of no-goods who may be easy to gravitate to. Unfortunately, they and their friends usually end up in trouble. Take care to avoid them.

There was no question that I should have avoided Steve.

Bakersfield wasn't exactly the trendy Sunset Strip of Los Angeles, but it wasn't Barstow either. Steve had a big, old, only-in-California heap of a Chrysler that he drove with pure abandon. He was fuming mad when we left the base that Friday afternoon, since he'd had his locker pried open and seventy dollars was missing. He was determined to get it back. Steve felt that the world owed him seventy dollars.

The trip was marked by a harrowing introduction to the Tehachapi Pass in pea soup fog. Steve was doing sixty miles per hour through the switchbacks, blasting the radio, and drinking a beer. I would have felt more secure walking into a barrage of incoming without a helmet or flak jacket. Coming down the west side of the pass, we caught the first sight of the sprawl that was Bakersfield—as unappealing in appearance as any place I'd seen. It did not improve as we got closer.

We spent the weekend hanging out with Steve's friends. "Hanging out" was a new concept for me. We had had little free time during the previous seven months, but even before then it had been a luxury I'd rarely been permitted. Time at Andover was tightly structured, and to my mother, idle hands really were the devil's workshop.

But that Saturday, hanging out, Steve and his friends talked about cars and girls—each with a level of familiarity that left me dumbstruck. It all seemed so free and open, so California. One of his friends talked about how he had gotten some new mag wheels for his GTO early the previous Sunday morning. He had simply backed his truck through the plate glass window of the display floor, thrown the wheels into the truck, and driven off.

"Why would anyone ever pay for mag wheels?" he asked no one in particular. Then, turning a glance in my direction, he said, "Jack, you need some mag wheels? I'll get you some. No shit. I'll get you some—come back with Steve next weekend and I'll have 'em here waiting for you. Right here."

"Ah, gee. Well, thanks. Yeah, thanks, but I mean, I don't have a car," I replied, or perhaps stammered.

"Bummer. Hey, I'll get 'em anyway and then you can sell them to someone back on base—get a couple hundred bucks— more than you can make in a month."

"No, thanks. I don't think they'd fit in my locker."

My feeble attempt at humor was lost on this group.

That night Steve and I drove into L.A. It was my first visit. We hung out looking for a party and then cruised the Sunset Strip in his big old car. It was sort of cool to be there, but I really didn't get it. I had a lot to learn about hanging out and cruising. Late in the evening, Steve stopped across from a liquor store and ran in to get some cigarettes while I waited in the car. Two minutes later, he came running out, jumped into the car, and stepped on the gas. I'm not sure that he touched the brake in the two hours that it took to get back to Bakersfield. Along the way, he reached under his white T-shirt and pulled a .45 caliber pistol from the waistband of his blue jeans.

A .45, for chrissakes.

"Where in the fuck did you get that, man?" I asked in total disbelief.

"'Sokay, man. It's mine. You know, mine from base."

"I can't believe you took that off base, Steve! Steve—they could court-martial you for that!"

"Yeah, shit, I know," he said. "Hey, sorry if I put you in a tough position. Really, Jack, I'm really sorry."

"What did you just do? Wait, what did you do in there? Oh, shit. I'm almost afraid to ask."

"Here. Hold this." Without waiting for my response, he took his hands off the wheel as I grabbed it. The Chrysler lurched hard right before I brought it back into line.

With one eye on the road ahead, I stole a glance downward in the direction of his pockets, where his hands were disgorging wads of bills. He'd pull out a few, go back for more, pull out a few more, go back for a few more, until there were bills all over the front seat of the car. His foot was still heavy on the gas, and my hand was still gripping the wheel as we flew across the table-top flatness of the lower San Joaquin Valley at better than one hundred miles per hour.

"Looks like I'm about even. Should be at least seventy bucks there, don't you think?"

Seventy? There were tens and twenties and fives and ones everywhere.

"Shit, Steve. I'd say you're ahead."

"Yeah, could be. Here. Take some. I only wanted seventy. You can have the rest. I just wanted to get even."

By the time we had pulled into his driveway back in Bakersfield, Steve had counted out $237. I politely thanked him for the offer to share but took none of the money. Instead, I became totally focused on getting back to the base as soon as possible. I was, however, acutely aware that I was sitting next to someone who was cradling a fully loaded, recoil operated, magazine fed, self-loading hand weapon on his lap. Fully loaded for this weapon is seven rounds.

I prayed that he still had a full magazine.

The following afternoon, Steve and I silently made the long drive back to Barstow. It seemed as though the whole weekend had been spent in the car. We each knew that our relationship had changed. He continued to express remorse. I spoke up once, telling him only that he was lucky to be alive.

"What if he'd had a gun under the counter, Steve? What if he'd had a gun?"

Steve laughed a short laugh. "Hey, he didn't have a gun, Jack. It's okay. I'm right here, man."

I didn't see Steve much after that. We usually worked different shifts at the warehouse, and he went home to hang out every weekend. He later told me that he'd come up with a new venture—stealing surfboards. He and a friend would take a truck, drive down the coast highway, and steal the surfboards that people would leave outside the back doors of their homes.

"Jack, you wouldn't believe this shit. People just leave 'em out—it's not like it's even stealing. And it's like Malibu, you know. They're all so rich, they probably don't even notice that they're gone. Come on. I got some other ideas too. I'll cut you in."

"No, thanks, Steve. I mean, you know, thanks, but no thanks, man."

I spoke with Steve one more time a month later. He looked

hardened and tough and tired, a far cry from the sweet guy who had been my friend back at supply school.

"Jack. Stereos, man. Stereos. You know, after a few weeks, there weren't any surfboards left. We took 'em all, or people were wising up to us. Anyway, there weren't any left. So, well, you know, I tried the handle on the back door of one of these richie houses, and it was unlocked, so I stepped in a little, and there's nobody there. So I walk in some more, and there's this stereo sitting there, so I took it.

"Jack, it's a gold mine. It's not even like stealing. I mean, they leave their back doors open. It's like an engraved invitation. People are so stupid. Do you believe it?"

Months later, shortly before I left for Vietnam, I heard that Steve had gotten caught stealing stereo equipment farther up the coast and had been given the choice of going to the brig or to Vietnam. He'd chosen the latter.

11

IN LATE MARCH 1967, MY ATTENTION TURNED TO THE Boston Red Sox. The games would be my daily companion until October, with box scores in the paper every morning and a static-filled game on my little transistor radio most nights. It was a wonderful diversion from the boredom.

Originally from northern New Jersey, I had been raised a New York Yankees fan. During my Andover years, though, my fan loyalties had turned to the local Boston Red Sox. The transition became complete when my parents moved to Brookline, two trolley stops from Fenway. I found that I could go to a game on the spur of the moment, pay a dollar to sit in the bleachers, and then be home again fifteen minutes after the final out. It was heaven.

The Red Sox, however, unlike the Yankees, were awful. The spring of 1967 brought little new hope. The Sox had lost one hundred games in 1965, had finished ninth in 1966, and were again one-hundred-to-one shots to win the American League Pennant in 1967. On opening day, they beat the Chicago White Sox 5–4. That afternoon, there were 8,234 fans scattered about Fenway Park. Usually, an opening day victory such as that would have kept downtrodden New England baseball fans in good spirits until early June.

Several days later, however, a twenty-one-year-old southpaw named Bill Rohr, making his major league debut, came within one out of pitching a no-hitter against the hated Yankees in New York. Softly, talk began that this year the Red Sox might actually have the stuff to contend for the American League pennant. Perhaps this year *would* be different. The new manager, Dick Williams, promised a .500 season—traditionally an unachievable feat for the "Olde Towne Team." There were, however, several diamonds in the Red Sox coal mine. Carl Yastrzemski and Jim Lonborg were legitimate stars. So were local legend Tony Conigliaro and hard-hitting shortstop Rico Petrocelli. Rookies Reggie Smith and Mike Andrews added to the promise of the dawning spring.

As it turned out, this year *was* different. In the words of *Boston Globe* columnist Dan Shaughnessy, "Across most of America this was remembered as the Summer of Love, the Summer of Sgt. Pepper's, and the summer of the Vietnam War escalation, but for young Red Sox fans it was the summer of the Impossible Dream." By the time I shipped out in October, my Red Sox would make it all the way to the seventh game of the 1967 World Series before losing to the St. Louis Cardinals.

On July 5, 1967, I arrived home in Brookline for several weeks of annual leave. It was great to be out of Barstow and wonderful to be home during the height of a beautiful New England summer. Despite the daily escalation of the war, I was nearing the halfway point of my enlistment and was increasingly certain that I would not go. A marine's tour in Vietnam was thirteen months, with another month of training prior to departure. I was running out of time.

On my first day home, I drove the twenty miles from Brookline to Andover to meet with Bob Hulburd, the school's college

admissions adviser. It felt good to be back on the sprawling campus. Much had changed in the past year. I felt taller. The school
seemed smaller.

I was certainly the only recent graduate to return as a United
States Marine. There was no bottom to the well of pride that I
felt. I was also becoming aware that my service in the Marine
Corps might actually be a positive force in the college admissions process.

I was excited about attending college and aspired to find a
suitable one near home. Boston University was an obvious
choice. Hulburd agreed. After further discussion, he suggested a
number of other possibilities and included Harvard University
on the list. He felt that they would be interested in my unique
experience.

In the early 1960s, with large thanks to Dean Bill Bender,
Harvard had broadened its admissions criteria. The university
then, as now, had little trouble attracting the top high school
students. The challenge became one of creating a balanced
learning environment. Bender initiated changes that gave weight
to prospective students who excelled in other areas—the best
oboe player, for example, or the best hockey player. Would they
give the same weight to a private first class in the United States
Marine Corps?

There was only one way to find out.

Hulburd thought it would be good practice for me to have a
warm-up interview before visiting Harvard the following week.
Although I was not particularly interested in attending college in
New York, Columbia and Harvard were similar enough that
Hulburd felt an interview at Columbia would be beneficial for
me. The day of my practice interview at Columbia, I pulled out
the gray suit—still new, still pressed—that I had last worn that
miserably rainy graduation day at Andover a year before. I
found a crisp starched white shirt and black socks in my father's
dresser, and a presentable tie in his closet. I removed my spit-
shined Marine Corps dress shoes from their flannel sleeves and
put them on to complete the outfit. The shoes felt awkward and

out of place without my uniform, but they were all that I had. The suit and shirt didn't quite fit, but I did feel well put together, considering the circumstances.

I walked out the front door, down High Street, and across Route 9 to the Brookline Village trolley stop and took the Green and the Blue lines to Logan airport. I made the nine o'clock shuttle to New York with time to spare and was sitting in the waiting room of the Columbia University admissions office in Hamilton Hall at ten-twenty. I was forty minutes early for my eleven o'clock appointment. As I looked around the room at the other candidates gathered for their interviews that morning, there was no question that I had the shiniest pair of shoes.

At the stroke of eleven, I was introduced to the interviewer. He was a short weaselly-looking young man in a black suit who, after leading me into his tiny office, directed me to sit on a cracked plastic guest chair. He positioned himself safely behind a large desk. My suit pants were strangling my thighs, which had bulked up during the past year. The early-morning excitement and my anticipation from the plane trip down from Boston evaporated in an instant.

He did not appear to be happy to see me.

"Good morning, Mr. . . . ah, McLean," he began as he fumbled to find my name on his appointment sheet.

"Good morning, sir."

"Let's see. . . . You're the person we got a call about from Andover the other day?" He was still searching.

"Yes."

"They wanted us to see you right away. I don't have any information on you. Is that your transcript that you are holding?"

"Yes," I replied, and silently turned over the envelope Hulburd had given me.

No small talk. No "So tell me what you've been up to for the past year." No "So how was your flight down?" He just wanted what was in the envelope. It contained my five-year Andover transcript and College Board scores. I should have spared myself the humiliation and just left.

"This is it? These are your grades?" He was mystified and made no attempt to hide it.

"Yes, sir."

I knew that he wanted to ask me if there was some critical piece of paper that was missing, if there was some obvious fact that he had overlooked that was key to my coming all the way down from Boston for this moment.

"Why are you here?"

I scrambled. "Well, I think that they thought you might be interested in my experience—you know, what I've been doing for the past year."

"The army?" He said the two words with the same drawn-out inflection that he might have used had I told him that there was an elephant in the room, which, I might add, there was.

"Well, yes. That is, the Marine Corps, actually, but yes." I decided to kill Hulburd as soon as I got back to Boston.

"Tell me, how old will you be at the start of your freshman year?"

"Twenty-one."

"That's going to be a problem. We prefer that our incoming freshmen be eighteen or nineteen years old. We think it adds to the camaraderie—you know, to the learning experience. It's the Columbia way."

The Columbia way?

Fuck the Columbia way.

Two days later, I made my way across the Charles River to Cambridge and historic Harvard Yard.

Again, I felt uncomfortable. My hair was short. I wore the same ill-fitting civilian suit over another of my father's starched white shirts and business ties. My spit-shined shoes reflected a scene that was light-years removed from the Parris Island parade deck. I could not have felt more out of place if I'd been wearing my uniform.

Yet the interview lasted an hour and I actually enjoyed it.

They had received my transcript, but that subject never came up. The young man who interviewed me, like so many others of that era, was attending graduate school for the purpose of avoiding the draft. He was, however, most interested in my experience and in me. He said that he admired my decision to enlist. He asked that I apply for admission. My feet never touched the ground as I left the office.

Before heading home, I stopped by the student store at the Harvard Coop and bought a crimson Harvard sweatshirt. I knew that admission would be a long shot but was pleased that I had made a good showing. I had no way of knowing at the time that that article of clothing would become the only piece of civilian attire to accompany me throughout my entire tour in Vietnam. Even on long midsummer patrols through sweltering jungle, the souvenir of my visit to Cambridge that day found its way into the bottom of my pack when perhaps an extra canteen of water would have been a more prudent choice.

In the end, I decided that I would apply to two colleges— Boston University and Harvard. I was thrilled at the prospect of attending either and felt that I had a shot at each. Were I admitted, I would be spending the four years after my discharge in Boston. Nothing could have made me happier. I wondered how I would ever survive another year of boredom in Barstow, but put the thought out of my mind.

The unlikely possibility that I might be back in Brookline within the week with orders for Vietnam barely occurred to me.

12

EVEN IN THE EARLY EVENING, BARSTOW WAS BLAZING hot as I stepped off the bus from the Los Angeles International Airport. It had been a long trip from Boston, and I was beat. With a seabag slung from my shoulder, I made the trek up the hill to the battalion office to report in with the officer of the day.

"Lance Corporal McLean, Lance Corporal McLean," he murmured as his finger scrolled down the duty roster. "Ah, Lance Corporal McLean, here you are." The young lieutenant looked up for the first time, and his eyes caught mine in a knowing gaze. "Lance Corporal McLean, you are to report immediately to Sergeant Enderly in the battalion office. I believe he has your new orders."

"Aye, aye, sir."

The blood left my face, and my knees withered as I picked up my bag and turned to go. All manner of possibilities flew through my head as I walked across the parade deck to the battalion office. Perhaps I was going to Philadelphia, but it did not appear likely. Every marine was a basic rifleman, and there was a war going on.

Sergeant Enderly was matter-of-fact when I appeared at his door.

"Lance Corporal McLean reporting as ordered, Sergeant."

"McLean," he responded. "I've got you right here." Piled carefully on the side of his desk were what appeared to be fifteen or twenty large envelopes all stamped with the familiar OFFICIAL ORDERS. THE UNITED STATES MARINE CORPS. He fingered down to the middle of the pile and produced the one with my name and service number clearly stamped on the cover. With aplomb, he stood and handed the envelope to me.

"Congratulations, Lance Corporal, you are getting the shit out of Barstow." With that, he shook my hand in a manner that felt more sarcastic than congratulatory.

"Where am I goin', Sarge?" I was sure I knew the answer, but I also didn't want to give him the satisfaction of watching me rip open the envelope and try to decipher the Marine Corps mumbo jumbo of numbers and acronyms inside. Sergeants took a vicarious thrill in the misfortune of junior enlisted men.

"They're going to make you a grunt and send you over," he replied curtly. "Adios, motherfucker. Be sure to write."

With that, he grinned and sat back down.

"Anybody else get orders?" I asked when I was again able to speak.

"Take a look," he said as he pointed to the pile on his desk. "Every one of you guys is going. I've been passing out the good news all afternoon while you all come back from leave."

Every one of us meant all of my supply school friends and then some.

"What about MacLeod, Sid MacLeod. Is he on there?"

"Yeah, he's here, but he's not due back for a few more days."

"Thanks for nothin', Sarge," I said as I picked up my bag and headed back across the parade deck to the barracks.

Many of the other guys had returned from leave earlier in the day and had their orders out of the envelope and under intense scrutiny. They laughed a gallows laugh when they saw me enter with the large white envelope in my hand.

"0311," I blurted. "Are we really all going over as 0311s?"

"Fuckin'-A right," responded Tom Ferguson, a short fair-haired private from Nebraska. The others nodded in quiet agreement.

We all had been ordered to report to Camp Pendleton to re-train as grunts—basic infantrymen. Like so many of our broth-ers from Parris Island Platoon 3076, our orders too now read "0311 WESTPAC." It seemed frighteningly real as I looked up and down the squad bay at the faces of my comrades to observe their initial reactions to being sent off to war, a war that was es-calating rapidly, building to what would become the bloodiest twelve months of the conflict.

Our timing could not possibly have been worse.

Camp Pendleton was a huge mass of large dusty hills spattered by low brush on the Pacific coast north of San Diego. We were stationed about twenty miles from the main camp at Camp Horno, the center for Marine Corps combat infantry training. Except for the three Special Infantry Combat Retraining compa-nies, of which I was a part, the camp comprised boot privates di-rectly out of the United States Marine Corps Recruit Depot at San Diego.

We were housed, three thousand strong, in an ever expand-ing tent city that sprawled up the side of a hill to accommodate the ballooning Marine Corps troop levels in Vietnam. The area around the tents was devoid of growth and inches deep in dust baked by the unforgiving late summer sun. It was incredibly filthy. Yet I was ready to be back in the real Marine Corps. I hadn't realized how much I had missed the structure and disci-pline.

The training was largely a repeat of what we had had at Camp Geiger. Here, however, we were all training to be 0311s and we were all going to Vietnam. We listened to our instructors more carefully, knowing that our lives now really would depend on our ability to read a compass and perfectly master each weapon. Yet, the more we learned, the less I felt I knew. I won-

dered to myself how in the world I would ever be ready in time
to join a combat infantry unit in the thick of the shit.

The feeling was surreal.

Though unrelated to my training, two events occurred in the
sporting world during my time at Pendleton that struck me. One
was the five-hundredth home run by my childhood idol, Mickey
Mantle. I had been alive for every one of those home runs—the
first player about whom that could be said. I felt I was getting
older.

The other was the decision by the World Boxing Association
to strip Muhammad Ali of his world championship title because
of his refusal to enter the military. It was increasingly apparent
that the white-bread American idealism of the 1950s, so well
represented by Mantle, was giving way to a more confusing
time, when sports, race relations, and the war in Vietnam were
all colliding in an enormous train wreck for the country. The
signs were all there. Ali's comment, when asked why he refused
to be inducted, was, "I ain't got no quarrel with them Vietcong."

Come to think of it, neither did I.

13

STAGING BATTALION AT CAMP PENDLETON IN CALI-fornia was the last stop for all marines ordered to Vietnam. Nearly six years to the day after sitting in the auditorium of Andover's George Washington Hall for orientation, I again was massed with a group of peers listening to valuable advice about my future. This time I was most attentive, trying to soak up any small pearl that might later save my life.

Each United States Marine headed for Vietnam in 1967 was required to watch a training film during the final days prior to embarkation. It was titled *Why Vietnam* and featured, among others, President Lyndon Johnson, Secretary of Defense Robert McNamara, and Secretary of State Dean Rusk. In it, they explained exactly why we were headed halfway around the world to a country few of us had ever heard of, to defend the United States of America against a growing ideology that fewer of us understood, let alone perceived as a threat.

"Why Vietnam," Johnson began.

I've never forgotten it. Even then—in the summer of 1967, when we believed that we could win this war, when we believed that our government was doing the right thing—even then, the film brought quiet laughs from many in the audience. Filmed eighteen months earlier, the celluloid propaganda already was out of date. The entire geopolitical situation in Vietnam, the United States, and, indeed, the world had changed, and changed dramatically. The war that I was heading to bore little resemblance to the war these men were discussing. The NVA were now an acknowledged power and arguably a superior force. Since the film had been made, 8,238 American boys had died. Not surprisingly, seven months later, Johnson's complete mismanagement of the war would force him from office.

Why Vietnam, indeed.

During the film, Johnson and his crew spoke of the domino theory. That is to say, if Vietnam fell to the Communists, then, like a row of falling dominos, Laos, Thailand, Cambodia, Burma, Indonesia, the Philippines, and God knew where else would ultimately fall as well. It was the middle of the cold war. The stakes were high. Around the world, missiles with atomic warheads bulged in their silos, itching for ignition. The Russians were Communists and bad. The Chinese were Communists and bad, but not friendly with the Russians, which made it confusing. The North Vietnamese, North Koreans, and Cubans were all Communists. Though the situation (save Cuba) had remained static for fifteen years, the United States of America had decided to draw the line in Vietnam. Unfortunately, as we would all learn later, the reasons that President Johnson outlined as causes for the invasion of South Vietnam were entirely fabricated.

One of the reasons for the war stemmed from an August 2, 1964, incident in the Gulf of Tonkin off Vietnam. That evening, the North Vietnamese Navy allegedly launched several unprovoked torpedo attacks on the U.S. destroyer *Maddox*, said to be on routine patrol. Two days later, after another alleged attack, President Johnson went on national TV to announce that he had ordered retaliatory action against the gunboats and supporting facilities in North Vietnam. The Gulf of Tonkin Resolution—the closest thing there was to a declaration of war against North Vietnam—sailed through Congress on August 7, 1964, with dissent from only Senator Wayne Morse of Oregon and Senator

Ernest Gruening of Alaska. The resolution gave congressional authorization for the commander in chief to "take all necessary measures to repel any armed attack against the forces of the United States and to prevent further aggression." It was to expire "when the President shall determine that the peace and security of the area is reasonably assured. . . ."

President Johnson had addressed Congress two days before, outlining his four reasons for escalation in Vietnam:

> America keeps her word. Here as elsewhere, we must and shall honor our commitments.
>
> The issue is the future of Southeast Asia as a whole. A threat to any nation in that region is a threat to all, and a threat to us.
>
> Our purpose is peace. We have no military, political, or territorial ambitions in the area.
>
> This is not just a jungle war, but a struggle for freedom on every front of human activity. Our military and economic assistance to South Vietnam and Laos in particular has the purpose of helping these countries to repel aggression and strengthen their independence.

The actual attacks were never proven. Most historians believe they never took place. In fact, the *Maddox* had been engaged in aggressive intelligence-gathering maneuvers—in sync with coordinated attacks on North Vietnam by the South Vietnamese Navy. The attacks were part of a deliberate campaign of increasing military pressure on the North.

But there were no gunboats. There was nothing there but black water and American firepower. Later the following year, it is said that Johnson admitted, "For all I know, our navy was shooting at whales out there."

Most do agree, however, that had it not been the Gulf of Tonkin incident, it would certainly have been something else. The United States was eager to draw the line against Communism and decided that Vietnam was the place to do it. Johnson had, in fact, drafted the resolution several months prior to the alleged attack on the *Maddox*. He had been waiting only for an event to trigger it.

As United States Marines, we cared little about politics or ideology. The actual cause was of little concern. Our commander in chief was sending us into harm's way for whatever reasons he saw fit. That was good enough for us. The less confusing the mission, the more focused our performance. "Semper Fi, do or die" was our mantra. We were going to go get us some gooks.

The "line" that Johnson thought he was drawing in Vietnam had been literally drawn fifteen years earlier. As a result of the Geneva Accords, the century-old French occupation of Vietnam ended in 1954. The country was partitioned at the 17th parallel of latitude. South Vietnam became the Republic of Vietnam and North Vietnam became the Democratic Republic of Vietnam. In the post–World War II world of realpolitik, not unlike partitioned Korea a decade before, the North immediately cozied up to the Chinese and the USSR. The South allied with the United States.

Ho Chi Minh, the premier of the North and the driving force behind the expulsion of the French a decade earlier, and his top aide, General Vo Nguyen Giap, the military genius responsible for the humiliating annihilation of the French forces at Dien Bien Phu in 1954, did not want Vietnam divided. Although the Geneva Accords had called for reunifying elections in 1956, an escalating dispute between South Vietnamese premier Ngo Dinh Diem and Ho Chi Minh allowed the date to pass. Ho Chi Minh had begun to execute his own plan for reunification that did not involve discussions with South Vietnam, the United States, or anyone else.

The American buildup in Vietnam began with several thousand military advisers that were sent in the early 1960s during the administration of President John F. Kennedy. The first major escalation took place in 1965 when a major force of marines made an amphibious landing just south of Da Nang on the northern coast of South Vietnam. By 1967, in an effort to interdict the flow of NVA troops from the North, major elements of the marines moved to positions along the 17th parallel, just south of the demilitarized zone that separated North and South Vietnam. One such position was a barren outpost called Con Thien. As the northernmost outpost in South Vietnam, Con Thien was in easy range of North Vietnamese artillery and troops.

Several months later, the defense of this small hamlet would become my first assignment in Vietnam.

During the six weeks prior to my arrival in country in the fall of 1967, North Vietnamese army gunners conducted one of the most intense artillery barrages in history, raining as many as nine hundred rounds of big artillery and mortar shells a day onto Con Thien—not a very big piece of real estate. The U.S. response included at least five thousand artillery shells and one thousand tons of bombs dropped daily from B-52s. The siege ended as the monsoons began and the North Vietnamese reportedly moved to higher ground.

General William C. Westmoreland, the American commander, called Con Thien "a Dien Bien Phu in reverse." He went on to say that Con Thien represented a U.S. victory, that the marines had taken the best that the Communists could throw at them, had held their own, and had fought back valiantly and effectively. It was, of course, an early instance of what became the American strategy in Vietnam: Declare victory and move on.

In retrospect, Con Thien turned out to be one of our first major blunders of the war. Had we learned nothing from the French? The Battle of Dien Bien Phu, fought in the spring of 1954, was the climactic battle of the First Indochina War between the French and Vietnam's Communist revolutionary Viet Minh. The battle ended in a massive French defeat that effectively ended the war.

During the battle, the French infantry had garrisoned themselves in the seemingly impregnable valley in northwestern Vietnam. It never occurred to them that the diminutive Vietnamese soldiers might be capable of hauling not only themselves but major artillery pieces to the top of the surrounding ridges.

Lesson one: Never underestimate the Vietnamese.
Lesson two? See lesson one.

A third lesson derived from the disasters at both Dien Bien Phu and Con Thien should have been to never again garrison large numbers of troops in a single position where they could become sitting ducks for enemy forces. This lesson, like the first two, had yet to be learned by the American commanders.

With the end of the siege of Con Thien, incredibly—almost incomprehensibly—the United States began the buildup of a small base in the foothills to the west. Khe Sanh lay strategically at an outlet of the Ho Chi Minh Trail, the North's major supply route. Alas, Khe Sanh also lay within easy range of the big North Vietnamese guns at Co Roc, Laos. The stage was being set for another major attack by the North Vietnamese on a stationary American target. It would come in the winter and spring of 1968 with a siege that would last 177 days.

Elements of the history outlined in the propaganda film *Why Vietnam* were familiar to me. In 1957, my parents had traveled to Vietnam on business and had been fascinated by the country and its people. I sat through hours of home movies of the Tet celebrations in Saigon, the endless rice paddies in the countryside, and the enormous rubber plantations controlled by wealthy (mostly foreign) landholders. Our home had numerous Vietnamese artifacts. The fact was, however, that to a United States Marine on his way to Vietnam in 1967, the history meant little. We were marines. They were gooks. We were good. They were evil. We had God on our side; they worshipped something weird.

We were trained to kill.
They were trained to kill.
This we had in common.

Late in October, we were informed that our flight would leave from San Bernardino early on the morning of November fifth. On the evening of November fourth, I found an available pay phone and made my last telephone call home. My parents tried to be positive. I tried to be positive. Neither side was convincing. I recall no genuine words of spirit or encouragement from my father, although he certainly must have tried. My mother showed no audible sign of the horror that she must have felt.

In my presence, my parents remained stoic.

My sister Barby was now fourteen—old enough to know what was going on and young enough to be really scared. She told me years later that she, Mom, and Dad just hunkered down for the year. A *National Geographic* map of Vietnam was hung in the front hall bathroom after I left. Week by week, a growing number of pins marked the movements of Charlie Company across the wide southern expanse of the demilitarized zone that separated the two Vietnams. Late evenings and early mornings would often find my mother or father walking sleeplessly through the drafty corridors of the grand old house.

I had bidden farewell to my parents many times over the years during my back and forths to Andover. I had, however, never said good-bye over the telephone. It was awkward, lonely, painful, and excruciatingly sad.

I made the long dusty walk back to the tent that served as our barracks. The sun was just setting. Before me lay a hundred glowing lightbulbs, each shining over the entrance to the ever increasing number of tents that stretched up the hillside. The marines inside my tent were reading, playing poker, and writing letters. Every several minutes, one would head off to or return from the pay phones for *his* last call home. There was little of our customary bravado or horseplay. In brief hours, we would begin our trek into the deadly serious business of war.

Early the following morning the buses arrived. The idling engines cut the predawn silence and brought me back to my arrival at Parris Island as Staff Sergeant Hilton rudely herded us into the musty South Carolina night. This scene, by contrast, was calm and orderly. One by one, we stowed our gear and filed aboard. We all looked exactly the same, dressed in green utilities with boots shined, heads shorn, and a faraway look in our eyes as our feet left American soil.

The moment was upon us. With a slow grinding sound, the buses shifted into first gear and began to roll forward into the predawn mist.

We were on our way to Vietnam.

14

DURING THE 1950S, MY FATHER WORKED FOR JOHN
D. Rockefeller III as an executor of Rockefeller's philanthropic
vision for Asia. This included creating nonprofit organizations
that would respond to the anticipated challenges in population
growth and food production. During my youth, my father was
often gone several times a year for weeks at a time. One such
trip was in February 1957 when he was accompanied by my
mother, John Rockefeller, and Rockefeller's wife, Blanchette.
Mom kept a journal of the trip in the form of detailed letters
home to us. A week of this particular trip was spent in South
Vietnam—ten years before my arrival there.

Her letter gives a prescient look at a country that, although
seemingly composed to her pampered eyes, was wired to blow.

Vietnam
February 4, 1957
Letter from Martha McLean to her children

I am sitting at the desk in our hotel room—my hands are already sticky hot and the sun is burning down on the Saigon
River outside our window. We leave at noon for Cambodia.

Along the river, people are hurrying back and forth, mostly wearing straw hats and carrying bamboo poles across their shoulders with baskets full of market things on either end. The women are the real sight in Saigon. They are tiny and beautiful. All of them wear very thin white silk trousers with a long tunic in every sort of color over it—high neck, long sleeves, and split up each side to the waist. They have sandals on their feet, and really stride along, their heads back, long black hair tied low in back and the tunics floating out around them.

Saigon is an elegant city. Wide streets, tall beautiful trees, and lovely buildings, mostly with high walls and gardens around them, and all painted a sort of biscuit color with red tile roofs, and flowering vines climbing around. When the French built here, they *first* laid out the streets, and *then* they planted the trees and last of all they built their houses. Now the French have gone—or most of them have—and the Vietnamese are running their own country. The President lives in a great palace that used to be the King's, and his picture is high on the front of most of the government buildings. Right now it's Tet, the Chinese New Year, and all the public buildings are strung around with lights. They call Saigon the "Paris of the Orient" and not only does it look French, but everyone speaks French too.

Because it's a new Republic (just two years since the revolution) and because it's the Rockefellers' first visit, everyone wanted us to see everything, and we have been escorted through hospitals, the University, the Museum, etc. with the people in charge anxious for us to get a good impression.

Last night was the final great event—a dinner party at the Palace. I found myself at the long dinner table seated on the left of the President with the Secretary of State on *my* left. Through the long procession of dishes the Secretary of State helped me with my chopsticks, cut my papaya for me, and we became friends.

The President talked a lot, and Mrs. Rockefeller managed him, so I wasn't *too* pressed to make conversation, but he gave me a great speech on how much he had admired Daddy (who had an interview with him *with* interpreter when we first arrived) so I was very proud. His name, by the way, was Diem, and he is regarded as a great hero here for the wonderful things he has done in South Vietnam since the Geneva Conference, when *North* Vietnam was given to the Communists.

There was lots of fighting before that, but now all is very peaceful, and while out in the country we saw tall stone guard posts along the road, most of the villages looked peaceful, with flowers, vegetable gardens, water buffalo hard at work and people hurrying busily all around. We visited a refugee center about fifty miles north, and saw many others along the way. They are all built around a big Catholic church. When the Communists took over North Vietnam it was the local priest in every town who led his villagers to safety across the border. They brought only what they could carry, and burnt all their houses behind them so the Communists wouldn't get them! Then *walked,* most of them, hundreds of miles. This country is only 10% Christian, but of course the priest let anyone who wanted come with him, and now each village has set up its own schools in the south.

All of them, men and women from the North wear black silk trousers and dark red tunics, so you can always tell which ones they are. Everyone starts the day very early, when it's a *bit* cooler, and *then siesta* for three hours at noon, and no afternoon school for any children! Dinner isn't until about nine in the evening when it's almost cool enough to be a little hungry. We can't eat any salad or fresh things here, except fruit that has the skin on, and we have little pills we have to put into the water, but mostly we drink wine and beer.

The Tet celebrations involved wonderful doings, with a

great colored paper dragon the main attraction, and boys beating drums, and dancing round going through furious whirlings up on high poles, his long flowing silk tail twitching around behind him. Everyone gathers around shouting, and it seems the point is for the demon to catch the evil spirit, so all will have good luck for the New Year.

Now we are in a plane again, flying to Phnom Penh, the capital of Cambodia, just one hour away. The country under us looks hot, and wet, and flat with *lots* of rice paddies and only a hazy sign of the mountains far to the north in the Communist part of the country. We are flying north, so maybe it will be an *hour* cooler at least.

While we were there a Hollywood group was at our hotel making a movie called "The Quiet American." There were a lot of them with Audie Murphy being the star. We watched them "shooting" two evenings—once in the market place where they had a great parade with dragon, lanterns and things, and another time right in front of the hotel, with Audie himself driving up in a jeep and coming into the lobby. The time of the movie is during the war against the French, so they had to hang French flags up everywhere.

We also had the "Fairless Committee" (Mr. Fairless is the ex-president of General Motors) investigating the American Aid program. They had eight Cadillacs—all numbered—to take them around the city.

Then just as we were leaving this morning an American military mission arrived to look into that *side* of the affaire but they looked rather dull by comparison.

Love,
Mom

Ngo Dinh Diem, my mother's dinner partner at the palace banquet that February evening in 1957, was assassinated on November 2, 1963, in a military coup that had the tacit approval of the United States. Three short weeks later, U.S. president John F. Kennedy was assassinated in Dallas, Texas. On that day there were sixteen thousand American military advisers in Vietnam.

When my parents visited Asia, the flight from Hawaii to Manila took twenty hours, with stops at Wake Island and Guam. The Boeing Stratocruiser in which they flew was an enormous converted bomber with two floors, magnificently decorated in what my mother referred to as "elegant pale blue, with coral-colored curtains" and pull-down sleeping berths. She called it "a flying palace." "I can't even touch the seat in front of me with my feet stretched out," she wrote. It flew at ten thousand feet with vivid views of the white-capped ocean.

> Now we're coming down, my ears tell me, and in a minute we'll see Saigon! Just three hours and we've had cocktails and lunch and a lovely smooth morning. I could go on! But I must powder my nose and be ready for the photographers at the airport.

My first flight to Vietnam from Okinawa, by contrast, was a comparatively short four-hour hop in a packed Pan Am 707 with several hundred fatigue-clad marines wedged shoulder to shoulder flying at thirty thousand feet—well above the ocean, well above the clouds, and completely removed from any hint of the reality into which we were about to enter.

My first sight of Vietnam occurred during our final approach as we made the slow bank toward Da Nang. I first saw the beaches—beautifully endless white sand beaches—followed by the emerald green of the jungle, bordered by a thousand rice paddies that stretched out to the horizon.

Vietnam seemed serene.

Timeless.

A thousand years of civilization lay simply before me.

Then we landed.

Instantly, the predominant color became red—red clay, red mud, red dust everywhere and all over everything. But at first there was a familiar feeling to what I saw. It was, after all, a United States Marine Corps base. All marine bases have a particular order and organization, whether in Barstow, Camp Lejeune, or Da Nang. The signs were all in red and gold; everything in sight—moving or stationary—had USMC stenciled on the side; people went about their business in a certain distinct marine-like manner. As such, Da Nang did not have the feel of a foreign country or a war zone. Looking out the small window, I could see that the marines weren't even wearing helmets or flak jackets. I felt relieved that we would not be hit by enemy fire upon disembarkation.

The evidence of the rapid buildup, however, was palpable. The airport at which we landed was now the busiest in the world. I was one of four hundred thousand American boys to set foot in Vietnam in 1967. The number would be considerably higher the following year.

A quick scan of the grounds revealed concertina wire, guard towers, tank emplacements, flimsy wooden barracks, and hundreds of tents. Parallel to our runway, we could see F-4 Phantom jets taking off without break, one after the other. The late afternoon sun reflected blindingly off the bright silver napalm canisters that hung heavily from their wings. Several of the jets carried equally devastating payloads of two-hundred-fifty-pound bombs as they headed off to provide close air support for a marine unit under attack.

For the first time in my life I felt trapped. I could neither go home nor hide. For a United States Marine arriving in South Vietnam in November of 1967, there were only two ways out—in a Pan Am jet from Da Nang, or in a body bag from the field.

I couldn't deny a twinge of excitement, however, as my foot touched the tarmac.

Our first stop was a large wooden shed on the edge of the runway. The inside was dimly lit by several fluorescent lights and was impossible to navigate because the tropical midday sun had temporarily blinded me. After several seconds, I discerned a long counter from which three lines of marines snaked around the room. At the head of each line was a sign hanging from the ceiling. Each appeared to designate a destination of some sort, although none was familiar to me—Phu Bai? Quang Tri? Khe Sanh? In my hand I carried a manila envelope with my official orders. I was to report to 1/4, the 1st Battalion of the 4th Marine Regiment of the 3rd Marine Division.

The 3rd Marine Division—Bougainville, Guam, Iwo Jima.

Iwo fucking *Jima!*

After several minutes of uncertain milling with my incoming plane mates, I was told that 1/4's base of operations or "battalion rear" or simply "rear" was currently in Phu Bai and that I should get in *that* line and arrange passage on a C-130 transport that afternoon. Phu Bai, I learned, was about an hour's plane ride north of Da Nang near the old capital of Hue. The pampering was over. A marine corps C-130 was not a Pan Am 707.

Back on the tarmac, we were herded up the C-130 rear loading ramp and directed to belt ourselves onto the benches that lined the bulkhead. The plane taxied, turned, and took off with a deafening roar that continued for the entire trip. The late afternoon sun shone brightly through the portholes onto the squinting faces of those who lined the starboard side of the fuselage. My back to the west, I stared across at them. They were all there—each stage of the Vietnam Marine Corps experience. About half looked as I did—brand-new fatigues, shiny jungle boots, pink skin, and, had I been able to see, they were ridiculously wet behind the ears. While we may have looked tough, trained, and ready, the fact was we were all scared shitless.

Anyone who tells you different is lying.

The other half was older guys—in tenure as opposed to age. Some were on their way back from R & R; others were returning to the field after having injuries tended to. All were frozen with the faraway trance that acknowledged that they were headed back into the shit. Their fatigues, boots, skin, and helmets were covered with the same dusty reddish-gray patina that covered their eyes and expressions. Between their knees were M16 rifles—scratched, scuffed, and nicked on the outside, but spotless on the inside. These rifles had shot at human targets and would soon again.

This was no longer an exercise.

I was to be one of them.

A basic Marine Corps hill humping, paddy sloshing, shit stir-ring, motherfucking grunt. Not supply. Not the air wing. Not guard duty. A grunt—the epicenter—the best of the best of the United States Marine Corps, the backbone of 192 years of American military excellence.

I was now Jack McLean, 0311, WESTPAC.

I quietly sang the familiar Parris Island cadence to myself:

One, two, three, four.
United—States—Marine—Corps.
This is—what we—asked—for.
Three—thousand—seventy—six.
We're the—best.
Of all the—rest.
Left-right-left.
Left-right-left.

I silently hoped—prayed—that I would remember half of what Staff Sergeant Hilton had taught me.

15

WE ARRIVED IN PHU BAI AN HOUR LATER, EARS RINGING. Several of us were directed to a truck that transported us several miles over a dusty rutted road to Camp Evans. We were then deposited in front of a vacated wooden barracks. Our unit, Charlie Company, was on an operation along the DMZ and would not be returning for several days. There were other new guys like me who, while awaiting the company's return, were passing the time with menial tasks designed to keep them busy. It was a letdown, but I was glad to make some new friends among the group. Three in particular, Terry Tillery, Doug McPhail, and Wayne Wood, remain friends to this day.

The first night was eerie. Lying exposed in an aboveground barracks, we could hear the steady sounds of artillery and air strikes all night long. We weren't yet accustomed to the sound difference between incoming and outgoing, or bombs, or artillery, or mortars. Hence, each explosion was a startling, potentially life-threatening event. Several boys who had already been there a day or two tried to calm the rest of us.

"That's an outgoing 105 mm howitzer," said one.

"That's a B-52 bombing five or so miles away," said another. And on it went.

Outgoing 81 mm mortar—night defensive fire.

155 mm artillery outgoing.

.60 caliber machine gun.

For the next year, noise would become our constant companion—outgoing mortars and artillery, incoming mortars and artillery, outgoing rifle fire, incoming rifle fire, Phantom jets, B-52s, 16 inch naval artillery, all stirred into a stew of sound. The same way one would learn how to sleep through the constant barking of a neighbor's dog, we quickly learned to sleep through all that was outgoing. We needed our sleep, after all.

Less than a week later, we joined Charlie Company in the field. This was it. All that we had learned since our first night of boot camp had led to this. We each had a thousand questions that were patiently addressed by our new leaders. Our lives depended on these leaders. They, of course, knew that their lives depended on us as well, and they were eager to respond to any small question or unspoken fear.

"Larry, I gotta pee. Where do I go?"

"Larry, where's my hole? Do I get a hole?"

"Larry, will I stand watch tonight? When? Who wakes me up? Who do I wake up? Which one is he?"

Terry Tillery was assigned to a fire team led by Buck Willingham of Maysville, Oklahoma. During the early days, Tillery occasionally felt that he had forgotten everything he had ever known.

"Buck, the wide part of the claymore faces out, right?"

"Buck, are we allowed to have rounds chambered in our rifles?"

"Buck, where do we get water, food? When do we eat? Where do we eat?"

That night we received our first incoming mortar attack. It was terrifying, even though I was dug safely into my hole. It sounded just like in the movies—a slow increasing whistling scream ending in an explosion. Other guys were scrambling all around, some even were laughing. For them, as it would soon be for me, it was routine.

Wayne Wood, Terry Tillery, and I were assigned to the 2nd Platoon. We quickly learned that we were not alone. Able, experienced marines were eager to help and would endure endless questions. The 2nd Platoon squad leader was Texan Robert Rodriguez, an exceptional marine who, like many of our new leaders, appeared to thrive under the pressure of combat situations. We listened carefully and learned well.

Every night the NVA would lob in a few rounds just to keep us honest. Occasionally someone would be injured, but mostly it was part of the daily give-and-take with the enemy. Our tender ears quickly learned to listen for the sound of the muzzle blast from the mortar—sort of a dull *thwump* sound. The first to hear it would yell "Incoming!" and all knew, given the high trajectory of a mortar, that we'd have ten seconds or so to find a hole.

We were mostly teenagers, full of bravado. We occasionally would yell back at them in defiance. "Hey, asshole, I'm trying to take a shit here," or "Where'd you fuckers learn to shoot, the army?" Every night it continued. Every night we'd taunt. We developed a whole subculture of humor to respond to the nightly visits.

Days before our arrival at Camp Evans, Vice President Hubert Humphrey had visited South Vietnam and presented the Presidential Unit Citation Medal to General Bruno Hochmuth, our 3rd Division commanding general, based out of Phu Bai. The citation recognized the outstanding performance by the division during the previous months. This included our defense of Con Thien during the siege. Days after our arrival at Camp Evans, we learned that General Hochmuth had been killed in a helicopter crash in nearby Hue—the old provincial capital. He was replaced by Major General Rathvon McClure Tompkins, who held the post until the prophetic arrival of Ray Davis in late May.

Shortly after joining Charlie Company at Camp Evans, we ran several days of routine road security along Route 9, the main east-west road. This involved watching endless convoys of marines heading west from Dong Ha to the remote firebases that lined the route. The farthest west of these was called Khe Sanh. I remembered seeing a sign that said KHE SANH back in the hangar in Da Nang. I previously hadn't heard of it, and wondered what it was.

The convoys would be followed by hundreds of Vietnamese women and children who swarmed about selling Jim Beam, marijuana, and sex. ("She virgin, give number one boom-boom.") It was difficult at first to discern our role. On the one hand, any one of these people could take out half the convoy; on the other hand, my fellow marines showed little concern, so as the new kid, I took their lead.

Within this context a most wonderful event occurred. After several miles of trucks and troop-laden tanks passed, I heard a familiar voice. My head snapped around to see the beaming face of Sid MacLeod, my friend since Camp Geiger, looking down from atop a passing truck. "Jackson. Hey, Jackson, how'd they let a second-rate supply guy get this close to the front?"

"Well, kiss my ass," I replied. "Look at you, all dressed up like a marine." My heart leapt out of my chest at the sight of Sid. I felt unbridled joy. He jumped down to the road and we just stared at each other. The encounter filled me with reassurance that I strongly remember to this day. Sid had been trying to get to Vietnam for a year, and now that he was here, he looked strong, focused, and happy. As strange and foreign as the whole scene was to me during those early weeks near Hue, the sight of Sid was reality. It reminded me that I was still sane. This friend from another time and place was seeing the same things that my eyes were seeing, and through his silent counsel, he was telling me that everything was going to be all right. This was what *he* had asked for. It was the happiest that I had ever seen Sid MacLeod.

With a lurch, the motors jumped back to life and the convoy began slowly to move forward. Sid grappled his way back up onto the truck, smiled, waved, and was gone. He was with

3/26, the 3rd Battalion of the 26th Marine Regiment. They were headed all the way west to Khe Sanh. We were headed all the way north to the DMZ.

We agreed to write.

Six months later, Sid was dead.

————

The following day, we began to get resupplied. It appeared that we were getting ready for a major operation. Word was that we were headed up to the "Firebreak"—a strip of land along the length of the demilitarized zone between North and South Vietnam that had been, under orders from Secretary of Defense McNamara, completely stripped of all vegetation. To the marines, it was affectionately known as the Trace. For the balance of my tour, our proximity to the Trace would be measured in meters rather than miles. Nothing living remained that way if it sat between us and the Trace.

We were the front line in a war that had precious few of them.

The early December weather was cold, cloudy, and rainy as we saddled up. We were choppered up to Con Thien, and then set off with Delta Company for the north. Our mission was to provide security for the Seabees who were building a road along the Trace between Con Thien and Gio Linh to the east. My every nerve and fiber was alert. The enemy could be anywhere and was certainly watching my every move. The old-timers spoke of their last visit to this area, where several boys had been killed and many had been injured.

"Right over there, McQuade. Remember? That's the old road down to the A Shau Valley," said radio operator Benny Lerma. "Isn't that where the gook with the RPG hit you last summer? The little motherfucker. I'd like to see him come out now. I'd stitch him from toe to head."

"You're such an asshole, Lerma. Shut up and keep walking or he'll stitch your ass," came McQuade's bored reply.

McQuade, a machine gunner from Baltimore, Maryland,

had been on the back of a truck doing road security. Years later, he recalled seeing a spot coming at him out of the corner of his eye. It was a rocket-propelled grenade that hit the cab of the truck before he could wince. The explosion killed the driver instantly. The other gunner succumbed to wounds later that afternoon. McQuade and the three others on the team suffered shrapnel wounds.

Our boys knew the terrain well and were eager for some payback. My strength grew with their confidence and bravado, but I hoped that the little motherfucker would not reemerge just yet. My first taste of combat would come soon, but I was in no rush to speed the process.

The first night was miserable.

The rain poured down, it was viciously cold, and there was no protection. Yet we were able to dig adequate fighting holes in the mud, fix the perimeters and lines of fire, arm the claymore mines, and set the watch schedule. As dusk settled, we sent two ambush teams and two listening posts outside the lines to wait and listen.

That evening, we ate cold, wet C rations and tried to find a dry spot to sleep. Most of us had ponchos, but they were of little use. The water running below us made the water from above bearable by comparison. The fighting holes quickly filled with rain. Our first priority was to keep our weapons and ammo dry, clean, and serviceable. Our personal comfort was a far distant second.

Enemy mortars found us early and stayed all night. None of us slept. The previous day had been spent humping up and down hills, through rice paddies, across the Trace, and into the far northern stretches of the DMZ. We had nothing left to give, but we kept on giving. There would be three more days of this—humping, digging in, setting perimeters, and lying in the rain until the sun finally came out and ever so slowly began to dehydrate our clammy bodies, clothes, and equipment.

The DMZ looked like the surface of the moon. There were huge craters from the B-52s and artillery strikes. A horrible stench of cordite from the bombs hung over the landscape. However, despite our location, despite the occasional incoming mortars, we were in fact fortunate to have neither made contact with the enemy nor taken any casualties.

We changed positions with the 2nd Battalion, 9th Marine Regiment on December 4. Holes had already been dug and lines of fire were well established, so the transfer was not difficult. That night was quiet. We sent out ambushes and listening posts, set out claymore mines and booby traps, and adhered to a normal watch schedule.

The following night, several squads from Alpha Company went out on ambushes, so we manned their lines as well. There was some movement outside the lines, several grenades were thrown by us, and we sent up the occasional illumination flare to see if we could see anything out of the ordinary. Alpha sprang both of their ambushes to little avail and, after igniting a green pop-up flare, safely reentered the lines around midnight.

The following morning, given the activity, we were put on full alert—my first since arriving in country. I carefully looked for anything that I could see outside the line and studied each of my fellow marines inside for guidance on how to react. This wasn't infantry training. This was the real deal. Here, as we had been told over and over and over again, mistakes cost lives.

Delta Company went out on a company-size patrol to the west and we stood their lines on the east side of the perimeter. All was quiet. We wrote letters home and cleaned our weapons. We could hear Delta Company, perhaps a thousand meters out, giving and getting small-arms fire and mortars. They returned several hours later. Near the end of the column, we noticed several marines carrying a body in a loosely wrapped poncho.

A rigid hand protruded from one side.

He was one of us.

He was dead.

My stomach turned and my heart began to race. Hours before he had been one of many heading off on a routine patrol, and now he was dead. I felt lonely, frightened, and very vulnerable. It could have been any one of them or any one of us.

Dead.

I redoubled my concentration to be certain that I was not missing any movement outside of the lines or an order within. All that I could do was rely on my training and those marines around me. That raised my confidence slightly, but had little impact on the unbridled fear that I felt.

Later in the afternoon, resupply choppers came in bringing mail and chow. I got a letter from my mother—my first from home—and devoured it. I read it over and over trying to extract every ounce of love and support that she could transmit.

The weather was chilly and damp, but it wasn't raining.

Suddenly came the cry of "Incoming!" We could hear the now distinctive sounds of the mortar tubing in the background. We scrambled for cover in any available hole, pulling as many fellow marines in with us as we could. After the first barrage, we scattered to our own holes to secure the lines against a possible ground assault. Terry Tillery, like me, was in his first two weeks with the company, and he jumped into a narrow neck-deep hole with George Randolph as the second barrage began.

"Incoming!"

The explosions were followed quickly by small-arms fire. Looking up, Tillery could see a large rice paddy stretched out below him with a tree line on the other side. The tree line was the source of rapid machine gun fire. As their mortars continued, we returned fire, but there was little else to do until the mortaring stopped. With that, Randolph pulled a poncho over the top of the hole that he was sharing with Tillery.

"What the fuck are you doing?" asked Tillery, incredulously.

"Well, brother," Randolph replied, "if you don't see 'em, it ain't as bad."

It was hard to refute the logic of the veteran Randolph. He had been in country for ten months and he was alive.

The small-arms fire then really started coming in all around the perimeter. I was frightened and disoriented, looking for guidance from any available source. The veterans appeared cool, so I just did what they did—stayed low in my hole and returned fire with my M16 in the direction of the incoming assault, which was, in fact, every direction. The mortars seemed to be getting louder and closer, so we stayed low but kept firing. I heard my first cry for "Corpsman!" Several holes away, an incoming mortar had landed next to one of our squad leaders. They began to work on him furiously.

A helicopter medevac was called for.

As the UH-34 helicopter slowly lowered to land, it was hit by a rocket-propelled grenade that took off the tail section. It spun wildly out of control for several seconds and then crashed right inside the perimeter. To those of us in our holes, it became increasingly difficult to focus with the escalating noise and activity. The helicopter was burning, the small-arms fire was incessant, and the mortars continued to come in all around with increasing accuracy.

In the midst of the attack, several of us were pulled back to stand in reserve, in the event that additional support was needed in a vulnerable area. Our orders were to stand watch and be prepared for whatever might happen. Being new, I had little idea of exactly what might happen or how I would know if it did. I was at once relieved and disoriented. Without a specific place to be and no hole dug, I found a bomb crater and lay inside, falsely believing that it would provide some security from incoming.

Expansive bomb craters, although deep, provided little protection from incoming artillery and mortar fire that came from high above.

An early lesson learned.

At dusk, another marine from the 2nd Platoon scurried up next to me to see if I knew what was going on. One look at his bright green utilities, new boots, and frightened expression told me a strange new truth: I was the salty veteran and he was the new kid. Whatever meager tidbit I possessed would be encyclopedic compared to his near complete ignorance of the situation.

I was scared.

He was petrified.

I was new.

He was newer.

He looked at me the way I looked at everybody else—like they were old veterans who knew exactly what to do all the time. To him I was the experienced one, so I acted the role and got the two of us through the most horrifying night either of us had ever spent. These were the circumstances under which I met PFC Dan Burton of San Diego, California.

Dan was California. He had a surfer's body and an easygoing manner that endeared him to nearly all he met. He was a solid marine and worked hard like the rest of us, but he played hard as well. He loved to laugh, smoke dope, and make wonderful spirit-lifting jokes at times when our morale was down. There were no jokes from Dan this evening, however.

The NVA were heavily probing our lines looking for weak spots. Delta Company was in the worst position. They had no fields of fire, and the enemy knew that. Within the hour, the enemy had penetrated the Delta lines.

"Gooks in the perimeter!" came the call.

As I had been trained, I removed my bayonet from its sheath and carefully fixed it to the end of my rifle. I tried to recall any useful morsel from my Parris Island bayonet training, listened for any sound, and studied the dark foliage for any unnatural movement. None occurred. The attack apparently was being repelled without my help.

I had yet to see the enemy, but I knew that I was getting my first taste of combat. Feelings of fear, excitement, and anticipation overwhelmed me. Yet the fear dissipated as the training and adrenaline took over. I wanted a piece of the little motherfuckers, but remained relegated to backup duty in my bomb crater.

The word then was passed that a radar-controlled bomb would be dropped just outside the lines to keep the NVA from overrunning us again. A radar-controlled bomb? This was not a weapon that we had learned about in training. The five-hundred-pound bomb was to be dropped from an A-6 jet in about five minutes. We would be given fair warning to be safe in our holes.

"Bombs away, thirty seconds!" came the initial call. There was not a sound from the air.

"Bombs away, ten seconds."

We could now hear the jet approaching, and then became aware of an increasing screaming roar from directly above.

Then it landed.

The impact ignited the night sky with an apocalyptic light. The ground beneath us shook ferociously, red-hot shrapnel flew like tracer rounds through the night blackness, and trip flares and claymore mines were set off by the concussion that exploded all around the perimeter.

Chaos was followed by horror.

The bomb had been dropped right on top of our lines.

The next sound, immediately after the explosion, was that of enormous pieces of shrapnel roaring inches over our heads and thumping deep into the mud on the far side of the crater. This was followed by the sound of what seemed to be heavy rain overhead. Seconds later, we realized that the sound was not rain but thousands of tiny pieces of shrapnel flying through the tree leaves, instantly denuding all that was in their path.

Dan and I remained frozen until we caught sight of several marines hauling five body-laden ponchos to the LZ (landing zone) for evacuation. One whole section of the Delta Company perimeter had been vaporized. As reserve forces, we moved quickly to cover the gaps in the line.

In two hours, we'd experienced a crashed helicopter, a friendly bomb, and countless casualties. Terry Tillery, still huddled with his fire team, felt himself starting to give up. He curled up, pulled his poncho tightly around himself, and quietly muttered, "Fuck it."

What could we do?

What were we gonna do?

It was bad enough that gooks were killing us.

Now we were killing ourselves.

Total confusion.

This was not a good place to be.

Despite its deadly effect on us, the bomb had succeeded in driving the enemy back, for the moment. Tillery emerged from his cocoon, Burton and I rose from the bomb crater that had become our home, and we all looked with disbelief at the battlefield around us.

The helicopter was still smoldering and the trees around the bomb impact either were gone or had been completely defoliated by the shrapnel. Our fellow marines were walking around with dazed what-the-hell-happened looks.

The word was passed to gather up our gear.

We were moving out, ASAP.

Gratefully, we packed up our gear, called in medevacs to take out the dead and wounded, and trudged two thousand meters back across the Trace to a position near Gio Linh, on the easternmost edge of the DMZ.

Within the relative security of the new location, I was able to write home.

Vietnam
December 8, 1967

Dear home,

Right now I'm sitting on the ground writing this on an empty C ration box. It's 4 P.M. and cold and bleak. The rain has let up for the moment, but the weather doesn't look good. Due to the casualties, we all have a bit more gear and more food, but none of us will ever be the same.

Please write if you get a chance—mail doesn't come often, but it's such a boost when it does. Don't worry about me; I am confident that I'll be all right. I'm sorry this can't be longer, but there is much work to be done.

Love,
Jack

Confident that I'll be all right?

I had no confidence whatsoever that I would be all right, let alone that I would see nightfall. My lesson for that day was that the line between life and death was random and arbitrary.

I elected not to share that revelation with my mother.

On December 6, 1967, the small group of us new guys had been officially baptized into the fraternity of combat-tested United States Marines. Although it was a rite of passage, it didn't feel that way to me. I hadn't killed anybody. I hadn't really even shot at anybody that I could see.

It had been eerie, frightening, invigorating, chaotic, and surreal.

Welcome to combat.

It was not like in the movies.

16

SEVERAL UNEVENTFUL WEEKS FOLLOWED. CHARLIE AND
Delta companies moved back and forth across the Firebreak
without incident, save the nightly mortar visits from the NVA.
The rain subsided. The sun came out. Although still cool in the
shade, it was almost warm, and we each grabbed every opportunity to dry our soggy gear and selves.

All agreed that there had never been a night like December
sixth.

On a quiet night weeks later, I was standing an uneventful
third watch thinking of home and wondering what the scene
was in Brookline. It was Christmas Eve—my first ever away
from home and family. A little before midnight, preparing to
wake my watch relief, I took a final scan out over the parapet
toward the desolately black DMZ beyond.

My rifle lay before me with a full magazine, a chambered
round, and the safety in the off position. There were several
hand grenades by my side—fragmentation in case they got close,
illumination in case I heard a scary noise. There was also a little
switch that connected to a wire that led to a claymore mine that
I had placed twenty feet in front of me. When activated, a clay-

more would eliminate all living things within fifteen feet of its face—plants, rats, humans. It was a nasty little weapon that provided great peace of mind to any weary marine on a late watch.

I had a fresh canteen of water and a half-smoked pack of Camels. I pulled one out and lit it—ever careful to shroud the ignition lest I expose my position. I was saving the remnants of a joint as a special treat for later.

I wasn't certain that I had ever been up at midnight on Christmas Eve. Dad and Ruthie used to go to the midnight church service sometimes, but I never found the idea very appealing. The faster I got to bed, the faster Christmas would come. I continued to believe that long after I stopped believing in Santa Claus.

Yet here we really were—caught in an unfathomably peculiar limbo between war and peace.

War—the previous two weeks had been cold, wet, mud, horror, death, wounded, scared, oh my God so scared.

Peace—a three-day Christmas cease-fire during which there was no noise, no movement, no patrols, no incoming artillery or mortars, and no outgoing.

At midnight, as I was preparing to give my watch relief a gentle nudge, a dull distant *boom* broke the silence. It was a distinctive muzzle blast from far to our south. Dong Ha? Quang Tri? Then another—*boom*. I thought it must be night defensive fire from the rear.

Why were *we* shooting?

More drumming boomed on top of the other. So much for Christmas. Then, all at once, the familiar whistling sound from far above was followed by a friendly pop.

A white illumination flare exploded across a jet-black sky . . . and then another. Alert. Senses spiked. Enemy activity? Eyes sharp, Jack. Adjust. Adjust. Use your peripheral vision. Look away from the lowering flare. Look for movement, any movement. Is the claymore still there? Yes. Thank God. Then again from high above a green flare ignited a sky that was already sprayed with a million stars, followed by a red flare.

A red flare.

Christmas Eve.

The silence of the cease-fire continued all through Christmas Day except for a brief early-morning flyover by a spotter plane with speakers that serenaded us with Christmas carols. It was very cool. No patrols were sent out, although the watch schedules were maintained. We took the time to breathe easier, while playing with children's games and toys that my sister Ruthie had sent—checkers, Slinkies, yo-yos, old maid, and Silly Putty. There were candy canes to eat and photographs of peaceful places back home in which to lose ourselves.

The yo-yos were the biggest hit. Machine gunner Tom Morrissey instantly made one of them his own. For weeks it never left his side. During an occasional quiet moment he could be seen alone pulling it out and, through the magic of a string and a round block of wood, removing himself to some distant New Hampshire childhood place.

Days later, Tom and I were on a patrol with the 2nd Platoon. I noticed him, far ahead where the column twisted around and into the tree line. He was at the edge of a rice paddy, kneeling to fill his canteen with the tepid swamp water. As he rose, M60 machine gun carefully balanced on his shoulder, Ray-Ban aviator glasses in place, he pulled the yo-yo from his hip pocket and with one downward thrust spun a perfect cat's cradle.

Then, with the flick of his shoulder, in a ritual of ultimate cool that he had performed a thousand times before, his weapon fell softly into his hands. In one unbroken motion he slapped a full bandolier of NATO 7.62 caliber ammo into the top, chambered a round, flipped off the safety, and followed his fire team back into the jungle.

Forever Tom.

I'm certain that no one saw it but me.

Six months later Tom Morrissey was dead.

....

A downside of the truce was that resupply was not permitted. On the upside, however, the word was passed that we would be moving out for a daylong march across the Firebreak to C-2, one of the McNamara Line listening posts, to stand lines around a bridge that spanned a small river just south of Con Thien. The word was that a hot dinner would be waiting for us, and, given the river, we all looked forward to our first bath in a month. It sounded like paradise and, as the boys of Charlie and Delta companies were to find out, for the next five months it was as close to paradise as a 0311 WESTPAC grunt could expect.

The hump across the Firebreak was hell. In one long day we covered the same amount of ground that weeks earlier had taken us three days. For once, however, the rumors were correct. The promised dinner of roast beef was waiting for us when we arrived—our first hot chow in more than thirty days. After nearly a month of C rations, our stomachs reacted with joy at the eating and with pain moments later as it rapidly flew out the other end.

The position was known as the C-2 bridge site. This differentiated it from C-2 itself, a separate artillery position directly to our south. The bridge site sat hard on a dusty rutted dirt road dubbed Route 561. The road was the north-south link between the village of Cam Lo to the south and Con Thien two thousand meters to the north. The bridge had been built several months prior by marine engineers in an effort to improve supply lines to Con Thien. The area was nicknamed "the Washout" since, during heavy monsoonal rains, the water flooded the low-lying ground. The terrain along the road consisted of low rolling hills and waist-high brush. It would be continually patrolled by us throughout the winter and early spring.

Our first assignment, in addition to patrolling and security, was to improve the shoddy bunker system that existed. According to the 1st Battalion's monthly chronology, none of the bunkers could be considered complete. We were joined by several support units—including engineers, artillery, and tank and antitank detachments—to both assist us and make mine sweeps along the road.

We ran constant patrols, but it was a quiet area with little activity. We could hear incoming slamming into Con Thien almost daily, followed by certain strikes on C-2 to our south. As an artillery position, C-2 was a more valuable target than our little bridge. When C-2 was being hit, we could hear the rounds coming over our heads from the north. It was eerie but soon became comforting. They weren't aiming at us.

Our first tasks, as always, were to secure the lines; create adequate fields of fire; set claymore mines and booby traps around the perimeter; and establish watch, patrol, ambush, and listening post assignments. This had become our nightly routine.

Over the next several months, every free waking hour would be spent filling sandbags and fortifying the flimsy bunkers. Soon, our noncombat gear was trucked up from Dong Ha and life became progressively more bearable. Hard rock dirt beds were replaced by air mattresses; ponchos were supplemented by light, quilted blankets; and the food and goodies from home finally arrived.

The sun came out.

We wanted for little.

Early in our first week at the Washout, I came across a copy of *Stars and Stripes,* the daily military newspaper. Starved for news, I read every word off the page, digested the sports scores, and scanned the comics. A small news item buried in the corner of the third page caught my eye. William Sloane Coffin, Jr., the Yale University chaplain, had been indicted by a grand jury in Boston on the charge of conspiracy to encourage violations of the draft laws. The charges were the result of actions taken at a protest rally the previous October at the Lincoln Memorial. He was subsequently convicted of the charges.

William Sloane Coffin.

Holy shit.

An iconic New England Yankee, Coffin had been my uncle Sid Lamb's Andover roommate. Coffin had gained increased notoriety both in the Episcopal Church and in the antiwar movement back home. Sid, not particularly religious, had enjoyed wondering with great humor what had happened during those Andover years to send Coffin off on such a celestial calling.

Any humor related to the Reverend William Sloane Coffin ceased the day I saw news of his indictment in the *Stars and Stripes*. Had it been someone else, it might not have caught my eye, but Coffin was so mainstream, so like my parents.

The antiwar drumbeats back home were increasing.

For the first time, we were beginning to feel them in the field.

17

WINTER AT THE WASHOUT PASSED IN RELATIVE TRAN-
quility.

On occasion we'd hear incoming and outgoing artillery from
the nearby outposts of C-2 to our south and Con Thien to our
north, but the NVA paid little attention to us. The bridge that we
were protecting had become increasingly inconsequential when
compared to the target-rich environments of our neighbors.

The lull in action brought subtle changes to our daily routines. Although patrols, listening posts, and ambushes went out
daily, and watch schedules were maintained, we could feel ourselves growing slacker by the day as the combat action of the
previous December 6 drifted into memory.

Our days were spent filling what seemed to be an endless
number of sandbags. The bags were used to fortify our bunkers,
reinforce the security of the ammo dump, and line the parapets of
the trenches and mortar enclosures that were also being created.

Heads were dug and redug. With all of us in one place most
of the time, we were running out of places to pee and shit. The
heads were outhouses, often two-seaters, with sawed-off fifty-
five-gallon drums under each hole. Once every day or two, a private or PFC would be assigned the unfortunate task of "burning

the shitters." This was accomplished by pulling the slopping drum from beneath the head, dousing it with kerosene, setting it on fire, and stirring it with a long stick for an hour or so.

Food came to us in two ways. Given the relative security of the Washout, one hot meal a day was trucked up from Dong Ha. Otherwise, all food came in the form of C rations. C rations were the constant in our lives—no surprises; we knew exactly what to expect days in advance. In an environment of uncertainty, where life itself could end in an instant, there was much to be said for this.

The uncontested worst meal ever thrown into a box was ham and lima beans—known affectionately as ham and motherfuckers, ham and mothers, or simply ham and moms. The only people on earth who seemed to like ham and moms were the Vietnamese. Perhaps they had developed a taste for it, as it was the one food that most marines used for barter, gave away, or simply left behind.

In January 1968, support for the war was still strong in the United States, although cracks were developing. On the evening of January 17, 1968, President Johnson stood before a joint session of Congress and delivered his fifth State of the Union Address:

Since I reported to you last January:

- Three elections have been held in Vietnam—in the midst of war and under the constant threat of violence.
- A President, a Vice President, a House and Senate, and village officials have been chosen by popular, contested ballot.
- The enemy has been defeated in battle after battle.
- The number of South Vietnamese living in areas under Government protection tonight has grown by more than a million since January of last year.

These are all marks of progress. Yet:

- The enemy continues to pour men and material across frontiers and into battle, despite his continuous heavy losses.
- He continues to hope that America's will to persevere can be broken. Well—he is wrong. America will persevere. Our patience and our perseverance will match our power. Aggression will never prevail.

Those of us in the field wanted desperately to believe the president's every word.

We still believed in what we were doing.

We still thought that we were stopping Communist aggression.

We still felt that the war could be won.

Although we remained out of the direct line of fire, evidence of the war was all around us. To better observe troop movements from the north, someone decided that it would be a good idea to defoliate the DMZ. One January day, we watched with curiosity as planes that appeared to be crop dusters began to spray the area north of us with a white powdery substance. Within several days, it was all over everything—in our eyes, in our rifles, in our water, on the leaves of every tree that we brushed by on patrols, and on the ground upon which we slept.

Agent Orange.

The defoliant of choice in Vietnam.

Immediately some of us began to itch. Others developed rashes. Over the ensuing years, legions of us would contract diabetes (myself included), have children with birth defects, and suffer all manner of physical maladies that could be traced directly back to the chemical dioxin—the active ingredient in both Agent Orange and napalm.

At half past midnight on Wednesday morning, January 31, 1968, the North Vietnamese launched the Tet Offensive at Nha Trang. Nearly seventy thousand North Vietnamese troops participated in this broad action that took the escalating war from the jungles into the cities of South Vietnam.

The following day, General Nguyen Ngoc Loan, a South Vietnamese security official, was captured on film executing a Vietcong prisoner, shooting him in the temple at point-blank range. American photographer Eddie Adams won the Pulitzer Prize for the photo. It was to become yet another iconic rallying point for antiwar protesters back home. Despite later claims that the prisoner had been accused of murdering a Saigon police officer and his family, the image called into question everything claimed and assumed about our South Vietnamese allies.

Over the following weeks, nearly every city and military installation in South Vietnam was hit. Even the U.S. embassy in Saigon was penetrated by enemy troops and resecured only after a fierce battle. The offensive carried on for weeks and was the major turning point in the American attitude toward the war. Little remained the same after Tet.

Throughout the Tet Offensive we could hear Con Thien and C-2 getting hit every day. The 3rd Battalion, 4th Marines, who took over our former position on the Firebreak, got hit by several battalions of NVA, and held their ground while losing only fifteen men. Choppers were on standby to take us up as reinforcements, but the call never came and we returned to our routines.

The Washout became one of the few marine installations untouched by the Tet Offensive.

Vietnam was not the only Asian country in which the mighty military of the United States was being tested by unconventional tactics during the early months of 1968. On January 23, the American military was brought to its knees by several North Korean patrol boats that captured the USS *Pueblo*, a U.S. Navy intelligence-gathering vessel, along with her eighty-three-man crew. It was the first time that a U.S. Navy ship had been hijacked on the high seas by a foreign military force since the War of 1812. The capture resulted in neither military action nor reprisals against the North Koreans. Their charges included violation of the Communist country's twelve-mile territorial limit. This crisis would paralyze U.S. foreign policy for eleven months, with the crew of the *Pueblo* finally gaining freedom on December 22, 1968.

Certainly the tepid U.S. response to the seizure provided a morale boost to the hordes of North Vietnamese soldiers who were quietly pouring across the border into South Vietnam, within miles of us, to commence the Tet Offensive.

What was up? we wondered. Those in command wouldn't let us go up to Hanoi to finish the job for which we'd been trained, and now eighty-three of our navy and Marine Corps brothers were being held somewhere in North Korea with the United States powerless to take action.

The United States Marine Corps was founded on November 10, 1775, in Tun Tavern in Philadelphia. Its purpose was to provide onboard defense to American naval vessels against the rising scourge of the Barbary pirates. Now, some hundred and ninety years later, we gave up a United States Navy vessel to a hostile foreign power without firing a single shot in defense?

Were *we* the paper tiger?

Would the United States government and Robert McNamara give us up as well?

It was beginning to feel that way to the boys of Charlie Company.

On Tuesday, February 7, Peter Arnett, a reporter for the Associated Press, went to view the ruins of the embattled South Vietnamese city Ben Tre. In his dispatch, he quoted a U.S. Army officer as saying, "It became necessary to destroy the town to save it."

To many, the quote became symbolic of the looming American failure in Vietnam.

Days after the beginning of the Tet Offensive, I accompanied a sergeant on a trip down to Cam Lo to get a situation report on some recent activity. Two squads from Delta Company had been sent down from the Washout the previous afternoon to bolster security following the NVA ambush of an army convoy.

We had stood lines in Cam Lo for several days shortly after my arrival, so I was familiar with the layout. Nothing, however, could prepare me for what I saw on this sunny February morning. Coming into the tiny village, we spotted six U.S. Army trucks on the side of the road, still smoking from the rockets that had leveled them the previous afternoon. Their frames were twisted. Several were on their sides. Blackened bodies lay in the cabs, burnt into the seats, all but irremovable.

We paused for a brief moment, and then moved on. There was nothing there for us to see and nothing there for us to do. As we drove around the corner, another horrific sight came into view. There before us was a pile of dozens upon dozens of dead bodies stacked as high as they could be thrown.

Gooks?

Yes, thank God.

The marines from the two squads of Delta Company that had come down from the Washout the day before to provide security were now methodically grabbing body after body off the barbed wire that encircled the small perimeter that they had established. The only sound was that of our idling motor. The only smell was the omnipresent stench of cordite—the detritus of modern battle. The bodies had been dead for only hours. It was a remarkably surreal scene—indescribable and instantly etched into my permanent memory.

Years later, I was sure that it had been only a dream.

The previous evening, those two squads from Delta Company had held off a vastly superior force of NVA that had targeted the previously defenseless Cam Lo village as part of the Tet Offensive. In one night, these thirty-five boys confirmed one hundred sixty NVA dead (with dozens of others certainly carried away). Enemy body counts in Vietnam were routinely inflated by the higher-ups. In this case, however, you could walk over and count them one by one. Thirty-five other NVA were captured, along with several enemy trucks and a flag signed by all of the troops that was to have been raised over the village after their anticipated victory. Delta Company had one marine die. Nearby, the army had lost several more in the passing convoy that had been ambushed in the beginning of the attack.

The entire scene was so far beyond anything that my sane mind could comprehend that, after a time, I forgot the incident but for recurring nightmares that continued for decades. Like many grunts, I had dozens of such memories that hung between the real and the surreal. They became part of our DNA. Therapy could bring some out over time. Most, however, were destined to remain right there, deep inside, as surely as if they inhabited a bone. They would not depart my body before I did.

A Delta Company marine, Corporal Larry Leonard Maxam, was awarded the Congressional Medal of Honor for his valor that night. It was awarded posthumously. The citation reads as follows:

> For conspicuous gallantry and intrepidity at the risk of his life above and beyond the call of duty while serving as a fire team leader with Company D. The Cam Lo District Headquarters came under extremely heavy rocket, artillery, mortar, and recoilless rifle fire from a numerically superior enemy force, destroying a portion of the defensive perimeter. Cpl. Maxam, observing the enemy massing for an assault into the compound across the remaining defensive wire, instructed his assistant fire team leader to take charge of the fire team, and unhesitatingly proceeded to the weakened section of the perimeter. Completely exposed to the concentrated enemy fire, he sustained multiple fragmentation wounds from exploding grenades as he ran to an abandoned machine gun position. Reaching the emplacement, he grasped the machine gun and commenced to deliver effective fire on the advancing enemy. As the enemy directed maximum firepower against

the determined marine, Cpl. Maxam's position received a direct hit from a rocket propelled grenade, knocking him backwards and inflicting severe fragmentation wounds to his face and right eye. Although momentarily stunned and in intense pain, Cpl. Maxam courageously resumed his firing position and subsequently was struck again by small-arms fire. With resolute determination, he gallantly continued to deliver intense machine gun fire, causing the enemy to retreat through the defensive wire to positions of cover. In a desperate attempt to silence his weapon, the North Vietnamese threw hand grenades and directed recoilless rifle fire against him, inflicting two additional wounds. Too weak to reload his machine gun, Cpl. Maxam fell to a prone position and valiantly continued to deliver effective fire with his rifle. After one and a half hours, during which he was hit repeatedly by fragments from exploding grenades and concentrated small-arms fire, he succumbed to his wounds, having successfully defended nearly half of the perimeter single-handedly. Cpl. Maxam's aggressive fighting spirit, inspiring valor, and selfless devotion to duty reflected great credit upon himself and the Marine Corps and upheld the highest traditions of the United States Naval Service. He gallantly gave his life for his country.

Corporal Maxam was just one of us. He had been a corporal, a fire team leader, a veteran of December 6, 1967. Until the day before, he too had been at the Washout, digging pissers, burning shitters, filling sandbags, and going on endless perimeter patrols. He was now the recipient of the Congressional Medal of Honor, as surely as if he'd been Audie Murphy himself.

Corporal Maxam could have been any one of us. This realization, and the horror of what our Delta marines had endured, snapped many of us in Charlie Company back to the reality that, although times were slack, the war was all around us, and in a matter of minutes we could again be in the very thick of it.

18

ON FEBRUARY 18, 1968, THE UNITED STATES DEPART-
ment of State announced the highest U.S. casualty toll of the
Vietnam War. The previous week they had counted 543 Americans killed in action and 2,547 wounded.

Early March brought changes back home that could barely
have been predicted even two months earlier. On March 12,
liberal Minnesota senator Eugene McCarthy, running on an
antiwar platform, came within two hundred thirty votes of de-
feating President Johnson in the New Hampshire Democratic
party primary election, the traditional beginning of the presidential campaign season. McCarthy's campaign was buoyed by
more than two thousand full-time student volunteers who cut
their hair, cleaned up their dress, and convinced the conservative
voters of the state that a new day was indeed dawning.

Four days later, Senator Robert F. Kennedy of New York,
responding to the abrupt change in the national mood, ended
months of speculation by announcing that he too would enter
the race to defeat President Lyndon Johnson for the Democratic
nomination for president.

The primary plank in his platform was opposition to the war
in Vietnam.

....

As winter changed into early spring, the days became hotter and the ground grew progressively drier and harder. What was left of the jungle had been severely defoliated by the relentless aerial spraying of Agent Orange over the past month.

We continued to feel ourselves becoming soft—losing our edge. We hadn't had any real sustained contact with the enemy since December 6, 1967. Half of Charlie Company had rotated back to the States by this time, and the rest of us were starting to get short in tenure and overly cautious.

When we returned to camp late one afternoon and dropped the deadweight of our gear from our exhausted bodies, we were greeted with the news that the commander in chief—the top person in our chain of command—was not running for another term.

The president of the United States, the near immortal Lyndon Baines Johnson, had become the latest victim of the war in Vietnam.

I have concluded that I should not permit the Presidency to become involved in the partisan divisions that are developing in this political year.

With America's sons in the fields far away, with America's future under challenge right here at home, with our hopes and the world's hopes for peace in the balance every day, I do not believe that I should devote an hour or a day of my time to any personal partisan causes or to any duties other than the awesome duties of this office—the Presidency of your country.

Accordingly, I shall not seek, and I will not accept, the nomination of my party for another term as your President.

But let men everywhere know, however, that a strong, a confident, and a vigilant America stands ready tonight to seek an honorable peace—and stands ready tonight to defend an honored cause—whatever the price, whatever the burden, whatever the sacrifice that duty may require.

The war had claimed its ultimate victim—the president of the United States.

The country was undergoing enormous change.

Nothing had a greater impact on this change than the now totally out of control American adventure in Vietnam.

What the hell were we doing there?

....

Early on the morning of April 5, 1968, as we dragged our filthy, smelly, exhausted bodies inside the perimeter through the south wire, fresh from an all-night ambush emplacement to the west, we were greeted with the most awful of the escalating bad news from home. The Reverend Martin Luther King, Jr., while spending a day working at the Lorraine Motel in Memphis to plan a Poor People's March on Washington, D.C., had been killed with a single shot from a .30-06 caliber rifle. Despite pleas for calm and a powerful extemporaneous eulogy from Senator Robert F. Kennedy, rioting had broken out in cities throughout the United States, rioting that had killed dozens of people and caused untold millions in property damage.

That morning, I became aware of a thin line that began to divide the black marines from the rest of us—nothing that ever manifested itself in combat, but a "something" that began to appear in a thousand little ways in our day-to-day lives.

19

The day that Andover seniors stood glued to their mailboxes to await decisions from the Ivy League schools.

Actual dates were of little consequence in Vietnam, so the date passed without notice, as did April 16. There were shitters to stir, sandbags to fill, and lines to man. I had no sense of time other than the gentle warming of spring. A supply chopper came in around noon on April 17 and off-loaded two large red nylon bags of mail, twelve cases of C rations, and several cases of ammo. I was eating lunch in the gun pit next to my bunker. Dan Burton brought over a handful of letters. Dan had a mad love back in San Diego and was usually among the first in the squad to pick up our mail from the command post. My mind was on R & R, which was two days off. I was hoping that my parents had sent a money order to help defray expenses.

I read the letters one by one—savoring each for minutes before turning to the next. I always got a lot of mail, and this day was no exception. The money orders arrived, as did a long letter from my father. Other letters came from friends and family filled with news and good wishes. The morale boost was incalculable. Near the bottom of the pile was a fat letter from Harvard University. It had been two years since I'd thought of the fat-thin differential, so I tore it open with no expectation about what might be inside, still smiling from the previous letters from home.

I pulled out a wad of folded paper. In the middle was a document with the Harvard University seal on top.

I had been accepted.

I had no idea what to do or say, so I said nothing for several minutes other than the repeated whisper of "Holy shit."

"Dan. Hey, Dan. You're not going to believe this shit." Dan Burton was engrossed in a letter from his girlfriend, but looked up briefly to acknowledge me.

"Waddayagot, brother?"

"Dan," I began softly, still unsure of the news myself. "Dan, I got into Harvard."

Dan got it.

His unconditional grin said it all.

He was as happy as he could be for me and was unabashed about showing it. First he gave me a hug, then swung me around, and then he commenced to share the news with all within earshot. To most of my comrades, he might well have been speaking Greek—such was their grasp of the concept of attending Harvard. Finally, Lieutenant Ladd, my former platoon commander, came by, put a hand on my shoulder, and said, "You know, McLean, it's not every day that a fuck-ass enlisted marine gets into Harvard."

He was right, of course, but I wasn't just an enlisted marine. . . . I was me, which . . . to me . . . made it even more unlikely. It took days to wipe the smile off my face. In Andover it was expected. Here, it was unheard of.

R & R was the most anticipated week of every marine's Vietnam experience. Those returning from their five days often remarked, not entirely in jest, that they would extend their stay in Vietnam for a year just to get another R & R. For teenage boys who had been in the shit for eight months and, for the most part, never slept with a girl, it was an exquisite experience beyond all imagination.

When one boy went on R & R, it was as though his whole squad went. Weeks before departure, every move and moment would be plotted. Most of the senior guys in my squad had chosen Singapore out of the eight or nine possible destinations. To leverage their considerable experience, I chose Singapore as well.

On April 19, I left the Washout on the morning supply chopper to begin a journey that would take me through Dong Ha to Da Nang for my flight to Singapore.

Arriving in Da Nang later that afternoon, I was overwhelmed by the changes that had occurred in the six months since my arrival in country. They were massive. The war was huge, and Da Nang was at the center of the buildup. Where tent cities had once sprawled, there were now wooden barracks. The dusty roads were paved. The PX could rival any stateside department store. I wandered around for hours feeling like a small-town midwestern boy seeing New York City for the first time. I could not have felt more distantly removed from the dusty little Washout.

We deplaned in Singapore the next day, two hundred uniformed boys representing all service branches, and were politely directed into an anteroom in which we were briefed about our five-day stay.

It's hard to imagine a more wonderful period than those first few hours of R & R.

The speaker was an army sergeant who somehow had swung the job of jobs.

"Gentlemen, there are buses waiting outside that door to take you to your designated R & R hotel. By agreement with the government of Singapore, you must remove your uniforms as soon as you arrive at the hotel."

This announcement was greeted by spontaneous applause, whistles, whoops, and laughter.

"Gentlemen, gentlemen," he interrupted. "I know you're all eager to get moving, so let me go over just a few announcements. The faster I finish, the faster I get you onto those buses."

Complete, utter bated-breath silence.

"The uniforms come off and the civvies go on. Each hotel has a shop in the lobby where you can buy the basics to get you started. The uniforms stay off until you get back on those buses at the end of the week. Is that clear? Please understand, you can be court-martialed if you're caught wearing a uniform."

This news was greeted by another spontaneous outburst.

"We want you all to have a good time this week. That's why you are here. Rest, relax, and enjoy all that Singapore has to offer."

More cheers, more whoops.

"Should anything come up which might require our assistance, please let us know. We're here to serve you. The office number is on the material you've been given."

"How 'bout bail bonds, Sarge?" The question was blurted out from the corner of the room.

"Let's just say that this is the last time I want to see any of you until you leave. That's it. Any real questions?"

There were several other questions, but mostly everybody knew the drill. After all, each boy had been planning his trip for months, deciding which city to visit, which hotel to stay at, and, in some cases, which specific companion to keep. Late nights during watch, we'd talk endlessly about where to go, what to do, what the air smells like. The stories were told over and over—tales to stifle the boredom of standing in a trench at three A.M.

There was no sadder scene in the field than the first sight of a boy returning from R & R. Soon, though, the stories would begin to pour forth and we would all revel in the wonders of Hong Kong, Tokyo, Bangkok, Kuala Lumpur, Sydney, Manila, Hawaii (mostly married boys), and Singapore—cities in countries that only months before had not even been in the vocabulary of most of us. Several weeks after a boy's return, the fervor would wane as the combat routine ground on and more recent R & R returnees assumed center stage with fresher material. By the third week back, however, squad mates would commence the ticking of a different R & R countdown clock.

"Last, but far from least, please be advised that the girls are required by law to keep their shot cards up to date. Be sure you check, gentlemen. The mama-san will help you make sure. It will save you a lot of suffering after you get back in country."

Venereal disease.

The clap, as it was called, gestated about thirty days after contact. It normally arrived in the form of an involuntary drip and painful urination. Those with symptoms would march up to see the corpsman and get a penicillin shot—some quietly, sheepishly feeling that God had given them their just reward for the first intimate encounter with a woman of their young lives.

For others, it was a rite of passage that let flow again the teenage bravado as the stories of the week's liaisons were validated. I recall the sight of Sal Martucci coming back down from the doc's bunker after his shot in the ass. He was struggling to pull up his pants with his left hand while stabbing his right fist jubilantly at the sky. A rite of passage indeed. Those fortunate enough to escape the clap in all likelihood contracted crabs or some other discomfort that would have them scratching their groin area for the balance of their tour. It didn't seem a big price to pay.

"Once again, gentlemen, be careful."

I was to stay at the Shangri-La Hotel and had been well prepared by my buddies. I had carefully positioned myself near the front of the bus to be the first off and, thereby, the first in the check-in line. When I arrived at the counter, I requested a specific suite, signed the register, was handed a key, and hustled over to the men's shop before the last person was off the bus.

Beach Boys music was being piped into the lobby.

Beach Boys music!

War? What war?

Having acquired five days' worth of presentable civilian attire, I headed for the elevators and the twenty-second floor. Once inside my room, I stripped off my sticky uniform, turned on the air conditioner, ran a bath, and sat down on the toilet.

Alone.

After six months of competing for crowded outhouses, rash-inducing bark covered logs, and other makeshift sanitary contrivances, there was an unspeakable joy to sitting alone on a real flush toilet. I closed the bathroom door because I could.

Nearly an hour later I stepped out of the tub, slowly turned to the full-length mirror behind the door, and viewed my whole body for the first time since Camp Pendleton. I was a sinewy sight, built in a manner that was unfamiliar to my eyes. My chest, shoulders, and legs were white. My arms and neck were black. My ribs were all visible. I stared, first in disbelief and then with growing recognition, at the boy before me. Once certain that it really was me, I opened the door, walked across to the bed, pulled down the covers, and flung myself diagonally across the crisp white sheets.

I fell asleep immediately.

When I awoke two hours later, the sinking sun was spreading an orangey golden glow across the floor and the far wall of the room. Where was I? My flak jacket. I felt naked without my flak jacket. Wait. Okay. Yes. This is okay. How did I get here? Don't I have to be somewhere? It's getting dark.

What time is my watch set to?

Quiet.

It's so quiet.

Realizing where I was, I sprang up, donned my new civvies, and headed down to the hotel bar. It was nearly empty. The mama-san was gathering up her things and heading out the door.

"Where is everybody?" I asked incredulously. "Am I in the right place?"

"Yes," the woman replied. "This is place. You late. All my girls go with GIs. You come tomorrow early and I give you number one girl."

Tomorrow?

While I had been upstairs taking a bath and napping, my fellow R&Rers had beat it directly to the bar and were now upstairs fucking their brains out. God damn it. Without delay, I headed to the taxi stand, bribed the driver well, and in less than an hour was back at the Shangri-La with—while not exactly Miss Right, she would have to do. There wasn't time to inquire about her shot card. By early morning, we had had enough of each other. She thought I was a crazy insatiable madman (wait until I tell the boys in the squad!), and with the dawning light I was finding her gold tooth to be a distraction.

My first full day of R & R was heaven. I walked all over Singapore, guidebook in hand, saw the sights, and went to museums. By midafternoon, I found my way to Raffles Hotel, a vestige of the British colonial rule, and had a Singapore Sling at the very bar where it was first served.

Conscious of the time, I headed back to the hotel, went directly to the bar, and had the pick of the litter. My gorgeous selection could not have been in sharper contrast to that of the previous evening. As we exited, I settled with the mama-san for the balance of the week and headed upstairs. As with most of my comrades before and after, I fell in love and swore that I would return to Singapore to claim my prize after my discharge from the Marine Corps.

The following days were a blur. We toured, ate in wonderful restaurants, and listened to the explosion of new music from back home—the Hollies, the Doors, the Beatles' *Sgt. Pepper's Lonely Hearts Club Band*, and Jimi Hendrix.

It was heaven on earth.

On the morning of my fourth day on R & R, while I was in the hotel newsstand to buy cigarettes, a photograph on the front page of the *International Herald Tribune* stopped me cold. It was a picture of the campus of Columbia University. Shown was the stoic statue of Alma Mater in front of the Low Memorial Library, the very symbol of the university. Hundreds of students were protesting on the Campus Walk. Several bearded, long-haired banner wavers were perched upon Alma Mater herself. One of them was giving the finger to the camera.

I was jostled by several of my buddies who pushed their way into the small hotel newsstand. We took a moment to recount the activities of the previous evening and to lay out our plans for the day. They were headed to the pool to nurse hangovers and suggested that I meet them there after breakfast.

I bought the paper and walked to the dining room. While being served a cup of coffee, I spread the paper out and looked again at the photograph. My Andover classmate Jim Kunen would be finishing his sophomore year at Columbia and, like many of my former classmates at colleges across the country, was certainly immersed in the antiwar activities that were beginning to explode across America's college campuses.

While I was deep into the Shangri-La of R & R, Kunen and others on the Morningside Heights campus were engaged in the unlawful occupation of five university buildings—the result of a demonstration against the university's involvement with the Institute for Defense Analyses. It had morphed into a protest over a new gymnasium. Seven days later, police stormed the buildings and violently removed the students, Kunen included.

It had nothing to do with Vietnam.

It had everything to do with Vietnam.

Bloating battalions of baby boomers were bursting the seams of every college in the United States. Here would manifest the ultimate expression of the generation gap that was becoming systemic throughout the country. A million boys and girls were in search of a means of expression—a way to be heard. Increasingly, that way took the form of opposition to the parent-created war in Vietnam.

Sitting in a hotel coffee shop twelve thousand miles away, remembering my own forgettable experience at the Columbia University admissions office months before, I was silently hoping that Jim Kunen was burning the place down. Well, not really, but I did feel validated to see that others viewed the university administration with the same jaundiced eye that I had acquired during my interview.

Kunen did not burn the place down, at least not with fire. The following year he published a chronology of those April 1968 hours in a book called *The Strawberry Statement*. It subsequently was made into a movie. Both did quite well. He was dubbed "a radical with a sense of humor." These were serious times. The mass market was thirsty for *anyone* with a sense of humor.

There was little humor, however, among most of the boys of Charlie Company when viewing the students involved in the uprisings that were beginning to take place.

They referred to them as "long-haired, privileged little shit-fuck draft-dodging motherfuckers."

None of us could believe them or understand them.

On the morning of the fifth day of my R & R, I donned my Marine Corps uniform, bade farewell to my companion, and headed for the bus.

It was the pits.

I was headed back into the shit, and it was getting hot.

Two days later, I returned to the Washout to find myself embraced by a welcoming throng of squad mates.

"Where did you stay?"

"Who did you fuck?"

"What did you buy?"

"Did you get some music for the tape player?"

My bunker mates couldn't get enough of every pearl that I had gleaned. As I started to tell them about the trauma of my first evening, I was immediately interrupted by Ed Finnegan.

"You asshole, McLean. Don't you ever listen to me? Didn't you hear me? I *told* you to get to the bar early. I told you that. Jesus."

Each brief story received similar interruptions. They could not get enough and they couldn't editorialize enough. It was, after all, their R & R as well. No detail, no matter how salacious, was too small or insignificant to be included.

The music and the tape player that I brought back became our constant evening companion for the next six weeks. We'd light the candles, fire up a joint, and lose ourselves in the new music of home.

Shortly after returning, I was promoted to the rank of corporal—my final promotion in the Marine Corps—and made a squad leader. I would now be either killed or discharged as a noncommissioned officer infantry squad leader.

Very cool.

I was every ounce a United States Marine.

The highlight of my return to Charlie Company from R & R was a rare letter waiting from Sid MacLeod. I knew that his unit had seen a great deal of action since the Tet Offensive, so I was relieved to hear that he was well and in seemingly good spirits. Like me, he had just been promoted to corporal and named section leader of his mortar squad. Having left an aimless college career to enlist in the Marine Corps, he wrote that he had now decided to attend the Wesley Theological Seminary in Washington, D.C., the following fall to become a Methodist minister. For the first time since I'd known him, he was excited about getting on with his life. As with me, late spring of 1968 was a time of burgeoning optimism for Sid MacLeod.

I wrote Sid back on May 7 and congratulated him on his good news. I went on to detail some of the more salacious experiences of my R & R, told him the Harvard news, and brought him up to date on our many friends that I had seen or heard of during my two passes through Da Nang.

I closed by writing: "I've got eighty days left, and you're close behind, I know. Stay cool, buddy, and keep the fuck down—we're over two thirds of the way home now."

The letter came back to me two weeks later stamped RE-CEIVED MAY 14 and UNCLAIMED, RETURN TO SENDER.

I sent it out again on the afternoon chopper. It was again returned a week later.

Then I understood.

Sid was dead.

Had he been wounded, the letter would have found its way to him. The Marine Corps was very good about mail. No, he had to be dead. There was no way to officially know, except to write our mutual friends in the hope that someone might have heard. Weeks later it was confirmed.

Sid MacLeod was killed in action from hostile enemy fire on May 9, 1968.

Sid was dead.

Dammit.

20

IN MAY 1968, 810 MARINES WERE KILLED IN VIETNAM and another 3,812 were wounded in action. It was the bloodiest month of the war for the Marine Corps. Of these casualties, none was from Charlie Company. Since the sixth of December 1967, we had been among the most fortunate marine infantry units in all of Vietnam.

It was under this veil that Captain William P. Negron reentered Vietnam to begin the second of what would become his three tours of duty. As with all marines entering Vietnam in 1968, he flew into Da Nang and reported to the 4th Marine regimental headquarters in Dong Ha. From there he boarded a jeep with a driver and headed fifteen miles northwest over dusty dirt roads to the 1st Battalion headquarters in Con Thien.

Shortly before arriving at Con Thien, the jeep came to a rise that was covered with red earth only—no vegetation. All the land to the north, for as far as one could see, had been completely defoliated with Agent Orange. Beyond the rise was a bridge that forded a nearly dry stream. Surrounding the bridge was the motliest encampment Negron had ever seen. There was a wooden watchtower and a conglomerate of shacks, bunkers, and trench lines that looked like a squatters' camp. He was incredulous to see evidence that it was, in fact, a Marine Corps outpost. Few of the resident marines that he saw were wearing helmets, flak jackets, or even shirts.

There was little sign of military discipline.

"What unit is *that*?" Negron inquired of his driver as they motored across the bridge.

"Charlie Company, Captain." The driver responded over the gasping engine. "That would be Charlie Company."

It was Negron's first look at the Washout.

He and his driver continued through the compound and then traversed the two thousand remaining meters north to Con Thien.

Within a week, Captain William P. Negron would return down the dusty road to become the commanding officer of Charlie Company, 1st Battalion, 4th Marine Regiment, 3rd Marine Division. Once again, Charlie Company was to become among the most fortunate marine infantry units in all of Vietnam. Without Negron's leadership, I doubt that a single one of us would have survived the coming weeks.

Bill Negron was an experienced marine whose previous life was unimaginable to most of us. Of Puerto Rican parents, Negron was born in the Bronx, New York, on November 10, 1937—the 162nd birthday of the United States Marine Corps. His mother was a sweatshop seamstress and his father a security guard. A scrappy Golden Gloves boxing champion, Negron graduated from the Perth Amboy, New Jersey, high school at age eighteen as the school's only Hispanic student.

The following fall, he entered Miami University in Ohio on a football scholarship. He was dismissed after only a semester. Returning to the New York area, he began a short-lived professional boxing career that concluded after his third fight in Madison Square Garden. He emerged victorious with a split decision, a concussion, a broken jaw, three cracked ribs, and a fractured right hand.

Six weeks later, he enlisted in the United States Marine Corps and took the train to Parris Island, South Carolina.

At the conclusion of his enlistment three years later, Negron felt that he was ready to return to college. Miami agreed. He graduated in the spring of 1961 with a BA degree in English.

Now, seven years later, Negron had attained the rank of captain. Negron's life had been filled with several unique experiences. His boxing career was only one of them. His first combat occurred not with the United States Marine Corps but with the United States Central Intelligence Agency during his senior year in college.

While home on Christmas vacation, Negron received a call from Frank Wright, his former Marine Corps platoon commander on Okinawa, who wanted to meet for dinner in New York that evening. Negron had high respect for Wright and had a particular memory of a comment he'd made one evening back on Okinawa.

"You know, Negron, there are at least twenty-three wars going on right now, and as long as we wear this uniform, we'll never have a part in any of them." The mood among the marines at the time was that the United States trained the best military, but refused to send them into war. Indeed, they had not been in real sustained combat since the Korean Conflict a decade earlier. Wright had been a lieutenant and Negron a sergeant. Other than that one encounter, they had not known each other well.

The two men met at La Guardia Airport.

Wright was now working covertly in some capacity and was recruiting people for a special project. He began the conversation by asking Negron what he thought about the increasing Russian military presence in Cuba.

"Well," Negron began, "if what they say about Russia planning worldwide domination is true, and Cuba is a threat to this hemisphere, what the fuck can we do about it?"

From that moment on, Wright did all the talking. He expressed two reasons why he was interested in Negron. First, he recalled that Negron had been an outstanding mortar forward observer. Second, Negron was fluent in Spanish. When they parted, Wright left Negron a card with a name and number on it, asking that he call whenever he was ready.

Two days later, as he was preparing to return to college, Negron nervously picked up a phone and dialed the number.

"Good morning. White Oak Investments. How may I help you?"

"Good morning. I'd like to speak with White Elk. This is a friend of his."

"Who may I say is calling?" The woman's voice was distinctly Latin.

"Just tell White Elk that Jersey Maid is calling and accepts his offer."

"Very well, Jersey Maid. White Elk will be calling you within the hour."

Minutes later the phone rang. It was Wright. He told Negron to return to school. He would be contacted and briefed there.

Negron completed the first semester of his senior year that February and made the honor roll for the first time. He then requested the following semester off to tend to "personal matters."

Two months later, on April 21, 1961, Bill Negron found himself shivering in chest-deep water off the coast of Cuba in an area that became known as the Bay of Pigs. He'd seen his first combat death the day before, and by morning had known that the American attack on Cuba would fail. The brave Cuban expatriates who formed the 406th Brigade were dead, dying, or being hauled away like animals.

Throughout the night, Negron had been screaming into his radio handset for the promised air support.

The response was silence.

He tried to contact the ship offshore that had dropped them off.

More silence.

Mortar rounds were landing all around, and machine gun fire was everywhere.

All of it incoming.

"Where is your fucking air support? Where are your naval guns? Where the fuck are you Americans?" Raul Sanchez, one of the Cuban émigrés who made up most of the invasion force, was livid and frustrated beyond all imagination. Suddenly, he raced out of the water and across a field toward a group of Cuban soldiers who were dragging members of the brigade to a waiting truck. He was firing his carbine from the hip and screaming. He was immediately shot and fell to the ground. Two Cuban soldiers walked over, one with a carbine and the other with a Russian AK-47. While Negron watched in horror, the one with the carbine shot Sanchez twice in the head and walked calmly back to the truck.

They had been in Cuba less than twenty hours.

Days later, after leading his small squad through escape and evasion maneuvers across the island, Negron was able to find a small boat, get away from shore, and finally make contact with an American ship. Several hours later, they were returned to Florida.

Two months later, Bill Negron was back in Oxford, Ohio, completing the second semester of his senior year at Miami University. Upon graduation, he was commissioned as a second lieutenant in the United States Marine Corps—one of the Corps' first Hispanic officers. His "semester off" was in the past and remained so for many years.

Participation in President Kennedy's disastrous invasion of Cuba at the Bay of Pigs was not considered a career-advancing experience for a junior officer in the United States Marine Corps.

The denuded red earth that Bill Negron first saw as he and his driver passed through the Washout on their way to Con Thien that mid-May day in 1968 stretched from the North Vietnamese border in the near north to Gio Linh and the South China Sea in the east, and Khe Sanh and Laos in the west. There were free and open fields of fire in all directions. The tactical terrain was apparent. Each commander had added to, improved, or simply changed his predecessor's plan of defense.

Begun as a squad-size observation post, Con Thien was now the command center of a reinforced infantry battalion, which included a 105 mm artillery battery section, an 82 mm mortar section, tanks, a water purification unit, various logistics sections from the 3rd Marine Division, and a sprinkling of South Vietnamese Army units who didn't appear to have anyone in charge. The rotting sandbags were an indication of how long the outpost had existed.

Prior to the siege of Khe Sanh, this little piece of real estate, a quarter the size of Khe Sanh, had been the target of North Vietnamese gunners for four months. More incoming had fallen there than on Khe Sanh during its entire siege. Con Thien had been the original northern outpost. Its purpose was to interdict southbound North Vietnamese men and supplies. The marine grunts stationed there felt that its only purpose was to provide target practice for the North Vietnamese gunners to the north and west. Each day squad-, platoon-, and occasionally company-size patrols departed the perimeter to go north, east, and west into the no-man's-land we called the Trace. It was, in fact, the so-called demilitarized zone that separated the North from the South.

During the day, the marines would make contact with the enemy. During the evening they would return to defend Con Thien. The lieutenant colonels who had commanded Con Thien had all been company-grade officers, lieutenants, and captains during the Korean Conflict fifteen years prior. They seemed comfortable with the defensive posture in which they found themselves.

They were good at following orders.

All this was about to change.

As Negron was arriving back in country, the 3rd Marine Division was celebrating a new commanding general who would be based in Dong Ha. His name was Raymond Davis, and he, like Negron, was appalled by what he saw. Offensive marines were in defensive positions throughout the region. The North Vietnamese skirted around them at will as the NVA headed to the more lucrative urban targets to the south.

Davis was determined to change all of that and knew that the only way to do it was to abandon the bases like Con Thien and Khe Sanh. He needed his marines back on the offensive. His simply stated strategy was to break the armed enclaves, put marines in the hills, in the jungle, and in the attack. He would emphasize mobility and movable firebases to counter the enemy buildup.

We were marines.

We were not trained to defend.

We were trained to attack.

We grunts were thrilled. Real leadership had arrived at last.

Raymond G. Davis was already a Marine Corps legend when he arrived in Dong Ha. A native of Fitzgerald, Georgia, he was commissioned as a second lieutenant upon graduation from Georgia Tech in 1938. During the Second World War, Davis earned the Navy Cross for extraordinary heroism while fighting on Guadalcanal and Peleliu. In Korea, several years later, he received the Congressional Medal of Honor for superb leadership, outstanding courage, and brilliant tactical ability in the face of overwhelming and insurmountable odds.

By his own description, General Davis saw himself as a man of action. "I never sit around and think about what others are doing. I am aware that, as a holder of the Medal of Honor, I belong to this nation forever, because of a combat situation where literally thousands of men's lives depended on the actions that I took when someone had to take action."

Davis became our division commander on May 21, 1968, and was quick to observe the futility of the existing strategy.

Within days, he had the Marine Corps mobile again, beginning with Charlie Company.

Negron and his driver eventually arrived in Con Thien after the long dusty ride up from Dong Ha. He dismounted, grabbed his gear from the back, bade farewell to his driver, and snaked his way through a trench line to the location of the battalion command post.

The underground room he entered had a curtain on one wall—apparently the entrance to the command post itself. Pushing his way to the other side, he saw a busy operations section apparently dealing with some current emergency. No one noticed his arrival. A company-size patrol on the north side of the Trace was heavily engaged. A short man was on the phone trying to get tank support. He turned and handed the phone to another man.

"Mike, you get Bravo Company ready to go. A heavy section of tanks will lead us out. I'll take the air officer and my radio operators with me. Be ready to go in five minutes. Move it." With that, he turned and reached down to put his combat harness on. As he was leaving, the officer looked Negron straight in the eyes and said, "Welcome aboard, Captain. I'll be back in a while."

And so was Captain William Negron introduced to his new superior officer, Lieutenant Colonel James H. MacLean.

Several days later, Negron received the news that Charlie Company, the ragged band of squatters that he had first seen from the jeep on his way north, was his. Having had several days to prepare himself mentally, he attacked his new assignment with enthusiasm and vigor. It was quickly apparent to all of us that a new day had come to Charlie Company. Although we were uncertain at first, we soon felt as though we were back in the Marine Corps and that Negron would get us back in the war.

It was a heady feeling and brought all of our dormant training and combat skills back to the forefront.

He began to spend time with every marine in the company—not just "Hi. How are you doing? Do you need anything?" time, but real time, over a can of C rations, or over a can of warm beer. He wanted to know about us and our families, our hopes, fears, and dreams. Quietly and carefully, throughout the process, he was taking inventory. Whom could he count on? Who had leadership talent? Whom would he want nearby when the shit hit the fan? He didn't have much time, but it was not a process that he felt he could rush. So he got to know a hundred eighty boys—one by one.

He was eager to check our morale and inventory our skills and experience so that he could bring us up to combat readiness as quickly as possible. He knew that he had only a few weeks to get us prepared for the 3rd Division's change in direction, because it had been decided that we would be the first to execute General Davis's new strategy.

On his fourth day, Negron took the entire company on a three-day patrol a mile out and around the entire exterior of the perimeter. Delta Company stood our lines while we were gone. He spent the time observing and, where appropriate, teaching.

How good were his officers?

Sergeants?

Squad leaders?

How skilled were the mortar men?

Who knew how to call in artillery?

Air strikes?

Naval bombardment?

Helicopter gunship support?

Hell—who could still read a map and a compass?

The following week, Bill Negron accompanied each platoon leader on his daily patrols. He saw that most of the men were proficient in the basic skills. They knew how to deploy the 60 mm mortars and machine guns and could call for air, artillery, and medevacs. And they did know how to read a map and a compass. They were weak, however, in preregistering and adjusting supporting fire on their patrol routes. These were necessary skills, critical to effectively reacting to emergencies that required artillery support.

Initially, the lieutenant platoon leaders quietly groused about Negron's presence on their patrols. They were the ones in charge of their smaller units. It was almost unheard of for a company commander like Negron to venture out on something smaller than a company-size patrol. Soon, however, they realized that he was not usurping their authority.

Then Negron began going on squad-size patrols.

Officers commanded platoons, but the squads within the platoons were run by enlisted sergeants. Egos were quietly deflated as all began to see that the Skipper, as he was known, wanted only to make us a solid unit. The early investment that he'd made in each of us on the enlisted side paid off weeks later in gold.

Pure gold.

Thanks to that, some of us are still alive.

After several weeks, Negron could feel the company coming together. He was earning the admiration of his lieutenants and, as a former enlisted man, was increasingly respected by the troops. But the actions that had earned the respect of his men were causing concern higher up in the chain of command.

One day, early on, he was called up to Con Thien to meet with Lieutenant Colonel MacLean, his first such meeting since taking over the command of Charlie Company.

"Captain," began MacLean, "you are not a platoon leader. You are a company commander. You will, therefore, not go out on platoon-size patrols. Do I make myself clear, Captain?"

"Yes, sir," replied a bewildered Negron, who followed with a respectful explanation of his behavior in the field. He didn't feel it was the time to mention the even smaller squad-size patrols that he had also been on.

"This, Captain, is a combat zone, in case you hadn't noticed, and not basic school. If your lieutenants can't handle a platoon-size patrol, they shouldn't be lieutenants or platoon commanders. I've lost enough experienced captains. I can't afford to lose any more. Your job is to stay inside the wire with the bulk of your forces. Do I make myself clear again, Captain?"

What an asshole.

Negron stood, came to attention, and said, "Is that all, sir?" The colonel nodded, and Negron was dismissed. He beat a hasty retreat south to Charlie Company. The two thousand yards may well have been two thousand miles.

MacLean never once came down to see our encampment.

Despite the pesky interference from above, Negron continued building Charlie Company into a formidable fighting force, while earning the gratitude of his men. He obeyed the order to avoid going on smaller patrols, but otherwise continued to thumb his nose at orthodoxy.

United States Marines in all wars have been notoriously ill-equipped. Vietnam was no exception. Our rifles, packs, boots, flak jackets, jeeps, tanks, and artillery were customarily outdated compared to those of our army counterparts.

We were at the bottom of the military supply chain.

Negron was extremely concerned about the prospect of taking us into battle with the gear that we had. Of particular concern was our load-carrying equipment, particularly the web gear and backpacks. The newer men still carried the old two-piece World War II packs that were designed for a midget and required a genius to assemble. Several of the veterans wore captured NVA rucksacks that were well suited for life on the move in the jungle. I had been most fortunate to inherit one a month earlier from a sergeant who was rotating back to the States.

Negron had been in the Marine Corps long enough to know that somewhere north of Dong Ha there had to be a warehouse full of packs and web gear. He also knew that there was no chance it would be a marine warehouse, given our historic supply problems. He called a meeting of the platoon commanders and unit leaders. He asked that we inventory all of our gear and come up with what would be required to go into battle.

Three days later, a jeep dragging an overfilled trailer pulled up next to the Charlie Company command post at the Washout. Emerging from his tent with some curiosity, Negron saw Corporal Dwayne Slate and Sergeant Smiley jump out of the jeep, pull the tarp off the back of the trailer, and throw all manner of equipment to the ground. By the time they were done, the two had off-loaded eighty-seven new nylon backpacks, two cases of load-carrying web harnesses, and piles of other vital paraphernalia.

"Where do I sign?" asked an overwhelmed Negron.

"Nowhere, I hope," replied a nervous Slate. "Take it easy, Skipper. Gotta go."

With that, the two marines leapt back into the jeep, made a quick turn, and sped back down the road toward Dong Ha. Negron shook his head as he marveled at the bounty. At that point, he noticed that the web gear boxes had United States Army stencils on them. He thanked God for Smiley and Slate, and for the United States Army.

Negron's hard work was beginning to pay dividends.

While he was lambasted and harassed by his higher-ups, increasingly his newly energized troops would go to any end to garner his favor. The new gear was but one example. Almost from the start, we adored him.

Late in the third week of May, Negron went up to Con Thien for a staff briefing with Lieutenant Colonel MacLean and his three other 1st Battalion company commander counterparts. He detected a new attitude as soon as he entered the perimeter. Marines were bustling about with purpose, weapons were being cleaned, and new equipment was being issued. Enthusiasm permeated the air. The operations officer called the meeting to order, and all stood as Lieutenant Colonel MacLean entered.

He looked tired.

"At ease, men. Here's the scoop. We're getting out of here. Division is abandoning all of these enclaves and going after the NVA where they are. Gentlemen, we're going to start fighting like United States Marines."

The four company commanders and others gathered in the bunker gave a loud cheer and began patting one another on the back.

Like the men they commanded, they were eager to fight.

MacLean continued, "The entire battalion has to be ready to move out in three days. Ordnance teams will be coming up escorted by tanks. They will level the bases as we depart. Starting tomorrow morning, the air force will begin extensive B-52 bombing along the Trace to the north. This is the real deal."

After receiving his orders, Negron headed back down the road to the Washout. He was excited, but also concerned.

Had his three weeks with Charlie Company been enough?

How would they do under fire?

The few who had been fired at with live ammo hadn't seen any real action since the sixth of December. We were excited. We were nervous. I took a moment to write my last letter home from the Washout.

Vietnam
May 24, 1968

It's now evening and the heat has become unbearable. It is difficult to write since my hand is soaking wet and drops of sweat are falling from my face onto the paper.

Captain Negron has proved to be superb. He doesn't get kicks from harassing the troops, as a result, most of our time is our own to do as we wish. We are all on fifteen-minute standby, however, just in case.

I've just returned from a Platoon leader's meeting. We are moving in a week to Camp Carroll over near Khe Sanh. The Washout and Con Thien will be abandoned. Camp Carroll is an artillery base providing support for the Con Thien and Khe Sanh areas. The count now is 64 days left in the field. The month of June should be a long and very hot one, but I am optimistic that everything will be all right.

Two days later, May 26, 1968, was my twenty-first birthday. Packages and letters poured in from all quarters.

I got enough goodies to feed the entire company, and so I did. Three days later, we saddled up to head south to Camp Carroll, which was located along Route 9, the main east-west corridor.

As we waited to depart the Washout, we watched our sister companies convoy down from Con Thien. Charlie Company would be the last to leave. The air was immediately filled with the sights and sounds of massive explosions to the north. We silently marveled as the smoke rose over what had once been Con Thien. One by one, the bunkers, trenches, motor pool, and old ammo dumps were blown by United States Army ordnance engineers. Three hours later, there was no Con Thien.

As we watched the trucks disappear to the south, we realized that, for this brief period of time, the one hundred eighty boys of Charlie Company were all that stood between North and South Vietnam.

Later in the day, we finally boarded our trucks and headed south. Departing the Washout, Bill Negron was again headed into combat.

Our first assignment, after arriving at Camp Carroll, was to handle road security along Route 9. The road was a scratch of a two-lane dirt road that would barely have made it to a map back home. The rolling hills that surrounded it were deep shades of green and yellow that changed to a greenish gray as the elevation increased. Despite its seeming inconsequence, the road was the main thoroughfare between Quang Tri and Khe Sanh. Scattered along both sides were the skeletons of trucks, jeeps, even helicopters—the detritus of past battles.

We were late arriving, and dusk was upon us. We were to relieve elements of the 1st Battalion, 9th Marines who were stretched out over six key terrain features that overlooked the road. Negron met briefly with his 9th Marine counterpart, Captain Mike Fuller. They briefed each other, studied maps, located artillery emplacements, and made detailed plans for Charlie Company's relief of the six emplacements. As they parted, Negron asked which of Fuller's companies was being replaced. Fuller's response presented Negron with the one challenge that he could not possibly have anticipated.

"Charlie Company," Fuller responded.

Charlie Company 1/4 was replacing Charlie Company 1/9. Two Charlie companies.

"This is going to be fun," Fuller said, and laughed.

"It's going to be a cluster fuck," said Negron. "I hope the NVA aren't watching." The sun set shortly after the first position was relieved. Marines of Charlie Company 1/4 got off trucks, and marines of Charlie Company 1/9 got on trucks. Each marine knew that he was in Charlie Company and each knew that he was in the 1st Battalion as well. Several, however, were unsure about which regiment they were in, as they were replacement troops who had arrived only that day.

The following morning, the sun came over the eastern ridge, the two marine captains stood just east of the Ka Gia bridge, shook hands, and began laughing. Though it had been one hell of a night, there had been no enemy action—no probes, no mortars, no rockets. All six positions had been successfully remanned the previous evening. During the next six hours, however, forty-one marines from Charlie 1/4 and Charlie 1/9 discovered that they were with the wrong Charlie Company. An exchange was made before noon.

The 1st Battalion, 9th Marine Regiment that we replaced that evening had earned the moniker "the walking dead." They had been in the center of every piece of heavy fighting for the last six months, from the Tet Offensive to the siege of Khe Sanh. Now it was our turn.

With the confusion resolved, the week providing road security along Route 9 became a productive time for Negron. Each morning the mail driver would pick him up and deliver him to one of the six scattered Charlie Company outposts. He would serve chow, deliver mail, and spend time with his marines one on one. Each outpost had its own personality and thereby gave the Skipper a rare opportunity to see small team units in action.

Early on the second day, Negron visited a position that was sited on a large hump-backed hill in the middle of a wide valley. The hill shot high out of the ground and, given its strategic position, probably had been constantly manned since the begin-

ning of the war. Sergeant Munroe, a veteran on his second Vietnam tour, greeted Negron along the side of the road and walked
him up the hill.

"No movement again last night, Skipper. All the bad guys
must have gone home." Munroe's broad smile could not hide
the devilish look in his eye. "You want a cold one, boss?"

"A cold one?"

"A cold beer?"

"Are you shitting me?" Negron was incredulous. "Where'd
you get the ice? Where'd you get the beer?"

"Ice is no problem, sir. Cam Lo village is right up the road.
For a few C rations, we get a lot of ice." Munroe pushed back
the poncho liner that served as the door to his bunker, reached
into a hole in the dirt floor, and produced an ice-cold can of Bud-
weiser.

They drank and laughed for several minutes and proceeded
to tour the compound. Munroe was a proud host. Every hole
was tied in with the next and they were mutually supporting. It
was a textbook defensive position. Munroe was a good combat
marine. He had his shit together.

"You know, Skipper, the last time I left Nam, I was a staff
sergeant. Two years back in the States and I'm reduced to
corporal. I come back here and, after a time, get my stripes back.
If there's a chance, I'd like to get my platoon back next."

"Munroe, you know things change in a hurry over here. If a
shot comes, you got it. Keep your ass down and take it easy."
With that, Negron returned to his jeep and headed to the next
stop.

The "shot" that Negron referred to arrived several days later
on the morning of June 6, 1968. Staff Sergeant Brazier, Munroe's platoon sergeant, walked into an enemy ambush with a
squad of marines. He was shot and killed instantly. Sergeant
Munroe became the 3rd Platoon commander shortly thereafter.

21

OUR FINAL STOP BEFORE BEGINNING THE OFFENSIVE
operation was again Camp Carroll, which was a large fortified
supporting artillery position along Route 9. We had just received
word that the choppers were on the way to move us out. Our
target that day, June 4, 1968, was a remote dot on the map
marked Hill 672 in the rugged hills south of Khe Sanh and hard
on the Laotian border. It became known as Landing Zone Loon.

We were well aware that we were heading into what would
be some of the heaviest fighting of the Vietnam War. We were
ready.

In late May, intelligence had confirmed that the North Vietnamese Army had infiltrated the 88th and 102nd regiments of
the 308th Division into northwestern Quang Tri province. Aerial photographs clearly showed a new road under construction
in the jungle south of Khe Sanh. It entered Vietnam through
Laos and ran parallel to Route 9 about twelve miles to the
south. At the time of its discovery, the road had already penetrated nearly twenty-five miles into South Vietnam and was on a
direct path to the city of Hue. An NVA tank battalion could be
seen staging while waiting for the road's completion.

The plan was to have us dropped onto a hill, have us secure

it on the first day, bring in artillery on the second day, blow the shit out of the area for several more days, and then abandon the position and move on to another hill to repeat the process. The objective was to frustrate the enemy, keep them on the move, and kill as many of them as we possibly could.

It was dubbed Operation Robin.

The first phase had us running road security along Route 9. We now were staged, with the rest of the 4th Marine Regiment, to begin the second phase in which General Davis's planned airmobile operations would be conducted south of Route 9 to destroy the enemy road. There was no question that we would be dropped into very hostile territory. The NVA had moved freely about this corner of South Vietnam for months and had built up significant troop strength and supplies.

Our reconnaissance had showed that they were everywhere above and, presumably, below the ground as well.

"After this operation, we're all going to be heroes and this fucking war is going to be over," crowed company radioman Terry Tillery.

The boast was aimed at Skipper Bill Negron, who was kneeling nearby in silent prayer. Terry Tillery was a nineteen-year-old lance corporal from Canfield, Ohio—a small farming community near Youngstown. He had signed up for a four-year enlistment in the United States Marine Corps exactly a year earlier. After five months of training, he was sent directly to Vietnam. He and I reported to Charlie Company on the same day in November 1967 and were both assigned to the 2nd Platoon. Tillery was a marine's marine—well trained, disciplined, and eager to take on any task that was thrown his way. He was quick to obey orders, but he also possessed the unique ability to think creatively and provide tactical solutions where others saw none.

Shortly after Negron's arrival in country, Benny Lerma, the company radio operator, rotated back to the States with his thirteen-month tour completed. Lerma suggested that Tillery succeed him. Negron agreed. Tillery turned out to be an outstanding choice.

This day marked only his fourth as Negron's right arm.

"Heroes, man, heroes," Tillery continued. "There's going to be a parade down Broad Street in Canfield. Me? I'm going to be in the lead Cadillac, and all the girls are gonna be screamin' and grabbin' at me. It's gonna be the biggest party ever. Mrs. Tillery's little boy will be set for life."

Even Negron, now engaged, was smiling.

"Oh, yeah," Tillery went on, noting the Skipper's attention, "the Skipper is going to be in the second Cadillac. After all, he is our leader. They'll probably make him a general and give him the Navy Cross. But—don't forget—the party's for me, and I get all the girls."

D-Day was June 4, 1968.

Our waiting at Camp Carroll was filled with the cockiness and bravado of a hundred eighty mostly teenage boys.

We were in good spirits, joking, nervous, and apprehensive.

"As bad as the shit's gonna be up there, the only cross we're gonna get is a big white one at Arlington," our artillery forward observer said. He was a realist. Still, we laughed, prayed, cried, were scared to death—every one of us—but kept up the bravado.

We believed in the cause and knew we would win.

We'd all come to fight.

None of us had come to die.

I was numb, feeling once again that circumstances were out-stripping my ability to process them.

Arriving at Parris Island nearly two years earlier had been frightening, but I'd gotten through it.

Arriving in Vietnam eight months ago had been surreal, but it had evolved into an edgy, but relatively safe, reality.

Now combat.

Real combat for the first time.

Like my fellow marines, I could only focus on the moment, keep morale up, and be certain that I was prepared. To that end, I cleaned my M16 rifle and filled each ammo magazine with twenty clean rounds. Two were then removed. The rifle seemed to jam less with the lighter load. I slammed one readied magazine into the rifle and evenly secured the others in pouches around my waist. The safety was clicked on, the action switched to semiautomatic. I cleaned my .45 caliber pistol; emptied, oiled, and refilled four magazines; and loaded one into the pistol. I chambered a round, clicked on the safety, and slid the weapon into the holster on my waist. I filled four canteens with fresh water and secured them in their pouches on my waist, next to the small pouch that contained a compression bandage and a bayonet, and the large pouch that contained a gas mask.

I rechecked the inside of my pack—four C ration meals, halazone water purification tablets, one claymore mine with detonator and wire, a clean pair of socks, two packs of cigarettes, four rolls of 35 mm film, a block of C-4 plastic explosive, two blasting caps, a fuse, bags of loose candy left over from my twenty-first birthday the week before, and a fresh box of .223 caliber rifle ammo. In the large outside pockets were stuffed four 60 mm mortar rounds. I tightened the straps, readjusted the harness for a clean fit, and buckled an entrenching tool to the back.

The chin strap on my helmet was rechecked to be certain it would hold through a rough landing. I placed a new plastic bottle of insect repellent securely inside the black rubber tire band that circled my helmet, and added a dirty little Harvard pennant to the other side. The helmet pennant had been my visible logo since returning from R & R.

My nylon pants contained a camera in the right thigh pocket. Two more packs of cigarettes were in the left pocket, along with a small roll of toilet paper. Other pockets contained a Zippo lighter and a five-dollar bill from my grandmother. She always sent five dollars on my birthday. I didn't know what to do with it, so I kept it in my pocket, where it wouldn't get lost.

Finally, I rechecked my flak jacket. One, two, three, four, five, six, seven hand grenades—four high explosive, one yellow smoke, one red smoke, and one willy peter (white phosphorus). The pins were securely intact.

On the ground, next to my pack, lay the four final components to my gear that would go on after I saddled up. They included my rifle, a 60 mm mortar tube, four bandoliers of machine gun ammo, and a LAW (light antitank weapon) portable rocket. All grunts shared the burden of transporting machine gun ammo, 60 mm mortar rounds, and rockets.

Satisfied that I had everything, I saddled up—web gear harness over each shoulder and secured in front; flak jacket vest slid on, zippered, and snapped. My pack was swung around and secured one arm at a time. I hung bandoliers, mortar, and rocket around the outside. My rifle was slung over my shoulder. I stood tall, stretched, felt the full weight, jumped, and wiggled several times to be certain all was secure, then slowly sank to the ground, knees first, while executing a carefully calculated roll that left me sitting—comfortably—propped up by my pack. I could sit like that forever.

I untied and retied my boot laces with double knots.

I was ready.

During the previous month, my thoughts at idle times like this had turned to my coming college life. While on a late-night watch, or filling sandbags, or burning shitters, I'd think of walking to class on a crisp fall day across Harvard Yard. I'd fantasize about meeting girls and going to football games. Occasionally I'd feel concern about competing academically, but since graduating from Parris Island, I knew that I could achieve anything that I put my mind to. I'd be sure to avoid math, however, just in case. As late May turned to June, most of my incoming classmates were just now graduating from high school.

There were no such daydreams this afternoon. The next hour would be the most critical of my life. The little free space in my brain was focused on the coming assault, setting up the perimeter, getting holes dug, securing ammo, and—well—surviving.

Harvard was a universe away and would remain so for the next six weeks.

22

LATE ON THE AFTERNOON OF JUNE 4, 1968, WE
heard the faraway sound of multiple rotors and knew that our
moment had come. Without a command or a single word, the
one hundred eighty boys of Charlie Company rose to their feet.
The only sound was that of groaning packs and straps. We readjusted to the standing position. Although choppers had been flying in and out of Camp Carroll all day, they normally came in
ones and twos, bringing supplies and mail from the rear, and the
wounded and the dead from the front.

This was different.

First came the familiar sound of one rotor, then two. Within
an instant the air was filled with a dozen well-spaced CH-46
combat helicopters. To the ear, it was a single near-deafening
noise as they lowered themselves to us.

"Charlie Company, 1st Squad, 2nd Platoon, I want two
fire teams in that first chopper with me. Tillery, Camacho,
Rodriguez—let's go.

"Move."

"Move."

"*Move.*"

There was a smooth urgency to Bill Negron's voice that both

calmed us and told us that this was it. As the first chopper settled down, its rear ramp lowered to accept our command group. Negron always made it a point to be the first person in the first chopper going into battle and the last person in the last chopper going out.

Always.

Within minutes, one by one, all twelve choppers had landed and scooped up an entire reinforced company of United States Marines who were headed to the last place on earth that many would ever see.

Those who did return would never be the same.

It was a prophetic beginning for the freshly minted offensive strategy of General Ray Davis. No more Dien Bien Phus. We were going after them where they lived. On this day, that meant west into the mountainous highlands that formed the corner of Laos, North Vietnam, and South Vietnam.

This would be the first hot landing that most of us had experienced.

We knew that the choppers would come under fire as soon as we were within rifle range, and that each of us would have rifles aimed at our heads the moment we disembarked. This was it—just like in the movies, except this wasn't a movie. As Staff Sergeant Hilton used to say, "This is as real as a hand grenade."

When our turn came to board, twelve of us ran up the ramp. We seated ourselves against the bulkheads across from one another on nylon mesh seats that were caked with the dried blood of previous missions. The crew chief and door machine gunner were eager to go. Chopper crews rarely were happy on the ground. The landing zone was hot. They needed us to bail out the instant the rear ramp was down.

After only seconds, the bird lifted and banked hard to starboard. Incredibly, I remained detached from what lay beyond. It was a beautiful afternoon. The sun was shining and the air was cool. We were well fed and rested. The countryside, from what I could see through the broken portal across the cabin, was lovely, green and lush. It might well have been New Hampshire on a

June afternoon. Soon, though, emerging into view from the
same portal came an otherworldly landscape, one that belonged
on the surface of the moon. There were craters upon craters
with no life, human or vegetative. The absence of vegetation had
become a common sight along the demilitarized zone between
North and South Vietnam because the region had been so thor-
oughly saturated with Agent Orange. Nothing could grow there
even if it wanted to.

But the craters?

This was Khe Sanh.

America's Dien Bien Phu.

For as far as the eye could see, there spread before us cratered
red earth. Some craters from the B-52 bombs were large enough
to hold lakes, filled by the spring rains. The afternoon light glis-
tened in the silver gleam as I watched the flashing shadow of our
helicopter dart across the landscape.

Khe Sanh.

Five months earlier, on January 6, 1968, General William
Westmoreland had initiated Operation Niagara to find enemy
units dug in around the lightly fortified Khe Sanh base and to
eliminate them with superior firepower. Eight French generals,
some veterans of Dien Bien Phu, were brought in to assist.

A week later, the North began an unprecedented artillery
barrage on Khe Sanh. It was the beginning of a siege that was to
last seventy-seven days. An early round set off an explosion in
the Americans' main ammunition dump. Enormous numbers of
artillery and mortar rounds stored in the dump were thrown
into the air and detonated on impact within the base. Another
enemy rocket scored a direct hit on a cache of CS tear gas that
saturated the entire base.

During that period, North Vietnamese gunners landed more
than a thousand rounds a day on Khe Sanh. American gunners
returned fire with an estimated 160,000 rounds of artillery during the siege. The U.S. bomb tonnage directed around Khe Sanh
was staggering. Air force jets had flown 9,691 tactical sorties
and dropped 14,223 tons. Marine Corps pilots flew 7,098 mis-

sions and released 17,015 tons. Carrier-based navy jets, some
redirected from missions over North Vietnam, flew 5,337 sorties
and dropped 7,941 tons. Air force B-52s flew 2,548 sorties and
released an additional 59,542 tons. The total tonnage dropped
around Khe Sanh was the equivalent of a 1.3-kiloton nuclear de-
vice *every day of the siege*. With the enemy strength estimated
at about thirty thousand, we expended more than five tons of
artillery and aerial munitions for every NVA soldier who surrounded Khe Sanh.

Not even this amount of unleashed firepower was enough
to calm the anxiety of American leaders in Washington. On February 1, 1968, General Earle G. Wheeler, chairman of the Joint
Chiefs of Staff, raised the issue with Westmoreland of "whether
tactical nuclear weapons should be used if the situation at Khe
Sanh should become that desperate." Westmoreland replied that
their use would probably not be required. However, he added
that if the situation did change dramatically, "I visualize that either tactical nuclear weapons or chemical agents would be active candidates for employment."

Nukes?

Good God.

The battle proved little. We abandoned the base after one
hundred twenty days, and the North Vietnamese immediately
directed their efforts elsewhere. Elsewhere, this particular day,
was to be the area around LZ Loon into which we were now
headed. As quickly as it had come into view, Khe Sanh was behind us. Our chopper banked hard to the port side and rose to
meet the looming foothills to the southwest.

"Thirty seconds, gentlemen. Thirty seconds."

The voice of the pilot snapped us back to our reality.

We were lowering fast and banking hard. We began to hear
the ground fire directed at us, each a small explosion or a metal-
lic *ding*. As the ramp began to lower, we again heard the voice of
the pilot.

"This is a hot landing, marines. A hot landing. Wish I could
stick around and have a few laughs with you, but I'm getting the

fuck out of here. We will not be landing. Do you understand me? The wheels will not hit the ground, but each of you will. I'm leaving in fifteen seconds whether you are off or not. Semper Fi, brothers. Go now. Go. Go. Go."

Go?

Go where?

Still above the treetops, we unharnessed and moved swiftly to the rear, waiting for one brave soul to make the decision that we were low enough to jump without breaking a leg.

The ramp lowered still farther.

We were each weighted down with fifty to seventy-five pounds of gear and uncertain about what a safe jumping height might be. But the first marine did jump, and the rest of us followed—landing hard, rolling—often onto one another. Loose mortar base plates fell around us, a .50 caliber machine gun tripod bounced across our packs, and cans of .223 caliber rifle ammo simply fell like rain. All had been kicked out rather than carried.

But for the sporadic rifle fire aimed in our direction, we were on our own. The rifle fire was, in fact, good news, because at least it gave us some indication as to where the NVA were. Otherwise, we were momentarily lost. We were on the slope of a steep hill enveloped in six-foot-high elephant grass that made visual directive impossible. We did hear voices.

"Miller's fire team, 3rd Platoon, hustle up, sound off."

Disparate responses followed.

"60 mm mortars—who has the second fire team tube?"

"Corpsman! Corpsman!" The call echoed across the side of the hill from several directions. Broken legs? Bullet wounds? Impossible to tell.

"Corpsman!"

All around us the other choppers hovered, discharged their human cargo, and left. Each wave of newcomers flattened themselves in the tall elephant grass while getting their bearings.

Then there was calm. The last of the choppers left, the shooting stopped, and we were left momentarily alone to gather our gear, our comrades, and ourselves. Lost children were reunited with parents. Lost luggage was reunited with passengers.

The hill we were on went up in one direction and down in the other. Taking out neither compass nor map, we headed up the hill. If we weren't the current occupiers, then we would be shortly.

When I reached the top of the hill, I had an unexpected encounter with Leeland Johnson, a friend from my time stationed in Barstow, California. Leeland was a squad leader with the 2nd Battalion, 4th Marines that we were replacing.

"Hey, Jackson," he said, and smiled. We briefly hugged, although we were so loaded down with gear that we were barely able to touch hands.

"How's it look, Lee?" I asked.

"Jackson, in a word, you're fucked. It's the hottest hill I've seen in country. We have succeeded in getting the gooks good and pissed for you . . . and I mean *pissed*. Word is there's a regimental headquarters under us." He pointed a finger directly downward for emphasis. "Like, down there."

Down there meant that the NVA were tunneled in directly under our position. With that and a quick wave, Corporal Leeland Johnson led his squad into the welcoming belly of one of the hovering choppers, which were now circling back to evacuate the forces we were relieving.

Our assignment was to replace the 2nd Battalion, 4th Marines who were already on the hill. It wasn't lost on us that Charlie and Delta companies were replacing four companies on a position designed for at least four companies. Bill Negron, radio operator Tillery, and the balance of the company command were the first to land. They were met by a young marine who escorted them along the ridge to a hastily fortified position. The rest of us ultimately got our bearings and made our way from more than a dozen separate drop points. We crossed the perimeter and quickly saw that the defenses were set for a battalion. Our two reinforced companies were half that size.

Negron was greeted by Lieutenant Colonel "Stub" Barrow,

outgoing commander of the 2nd Battalion, 4th Marines. They
shook hands as Barrow gave Negron a quick briefing. Barrow
said that two of his rifle companies had been probed heavily the
previous two nights. He pointed the way to the general location.
His other two companies on the high ground to the southwest
had received moderate probing. At that moment, the first enemy
mortar landed nearby. Barrow stuffed the map into Negron's
hand, wished him luck, and, with his radio operator scurrying
behind, boarded the last chopper.

"It's all yours," he shouted to Negron as the bird lifted
off, but the rest of his words were lost in the prop wash of the
chopper.

LZ Loon was a long knoll, about thirty yards by seventy yards.
It was covered with mostly low scrub vegetation that provided
little relief from the pounding sun, and no cover from the lurk-
ing enemy. The ground cover on the lower elevations included
eye-high elephant grass that made the hill's defense difficult. But
for the freshly dug marine fighting holes along the perimeter, LZ
Loon appeared to be untouched by the ravages of the war. It was
a beautiful spot. Given our elevation, the air was cooler than it
had been at Camp Carroll, and the views over the top of the jungle were breathtaking.

Delta Company had landed on an adjacent knoll one hundred yards to our north. Although separated by a deep ravine,
we were in easy eyesight of each other. To the south, large rolling
hills stretched for miles. To the east, the landscape dropped off
steeply into jungle. Our principal concern, however, was to
the west—the sharp ridges that protected the feared NVA artillery and rocket emplacements in Co Roc, Laos. Although
twelve miles away, these were the same big North Vietnamese
guns that had held nearby Khe Sanh under siege the previous
winter.

The landing had brought confusion. We had departed later

than planned, and so nightfall arrived before our 3rd Platoon could get in. We struggled to determine how the lines should be manned with our limited resources. Over the following hour, the troops were set in, lines of fire were established, holes were redug, and claymore mines were set out. Charlie Company occupied the low ground that two companies had previously manned. That meant we had roughly one position for every two holes. Although we were able to arrange overlapping lines of fire, we knew that if one of the holes was taken out, we would be extremely vulnerable to a ground attack.

Delta Company, led by the former Charlie Company executive officer, Lieutenant Mike Jackson, took the high ground to the north and faced the same manpower challenge. We had a 106 mm recoilless rifle in place—a devastating low-trajectory infantry cannon that was ideal for this situation. We also were supplied with a .50 caliber machine gun, perhaps the most awesome of all small arms.

The expected artillery rounds from Co Roc flew over us for most of the late afternoon of June fourth, missing their mark and exploding harmlessly in the valley beyond. We all laughed, of course. We recalled our recent experience on the flat plain of Gio Linh, where the NVA forward artillery observers who called in the rounds could rarely get one inside the wire. The idea of hitting a tiny hilltop from twelve miles away was, thereby, nearly unimaginable.

Still, they continued to try.

The mortars and guns quieted long enough for Negron and Tillery to make their way over to the Delta Company position to compare notes with Lieutenant Jackson. It was nearly impossible for them to navigate their way around the hill because they were blinded by the tall elephant grass. On their way, they saw two CH-46 helicopters laboring under the weight of several pallets of 105 mm artillery ammo that were being delivered.

"This must have been a major NVA position," remarked Jackson. "We've got log bunkers with connecting trenches leading over to your position." He seemed overjoyed. The NVA had done a good job, which would make our job that much easier.

Charlie Company, positioned on the lower ground, had evidence of a prior NVA presence, but our position was not nearly as fortified as Jackson's. The fields of fire were inadequate, with the elephant grass and scrub bushes coming right up to the fighting holes on several sides. The battalion had not designated a command group for the two companies together, so Negron and Jackson felt their way through it—"The artillery forward observer will go up here, the landing zone will be over there, and let's both keep a radio tuned to the battalion net so we don't lose anything."

A giant flying crane helicopter appeared carrying a backhoe and several U.S. Army engineers. It looked like a praying mantis. The backhoe was to be used to dig 105 mm artillery emplacements. Our job was to protect the base while they dug the holes and brought in the guns the following day. Once the artillery battalion arrived, we could begin our regular patrols around the perimeter.

As Negron and Tillery headed back across the ridge to the Charlie Company position, the mortar tubing began again. No rounds had fallen inside the perimeter as yet, but it was only a matter of time. Unlike the long-range artillery, the mortars were being launched from the woods nearby and, although not as devastating as artillery, could be made deadly accurate more quickly. By the time Negron and Tillery returned, the company gunnery sergeant had set up a company command post just under the crest of the hill and next to the only standing tree.

Within seconds, the first mortar round landed inside the Charlie Company lines about thirty yards from where Negron and Tillery were standing. The next round fell about thirty yards past the position. They glanced at each other with tacit mutual understanding.

The gooks were bracketing in on the tree.

If they didn't move, the next round would be on their heads. So they simultaneously screamed "Incoming!" and, grabbing every marine in their path, fled to a nearby hole. Seconds later it came—*KABOOM*—right on the tree. Then came another, and then another all on exactly the same spot.

It was now apparent that the NVA forward observer had been using the tree as a focused target for the mortars, so that he could triangulate the grid for the artillery, twelve miles away. The mortars were meant to be little more than spotter rounds to determine precise coordinates.

I thought I had seen the mortar setup. Dan Burton and I were taking a breather while digging our holes and looked out across to the adjacent wooded ridge several hundred yards away. We noticed two men entering a small clearing. Was it the NVA? If it was, it was the first time in my tour that I had seen an NVA soldier in the open. Not a good sign. If they were in the open, it meant there was no room in the woods. Wasn't Delta over there? We were still becoming oriented to our new position. Moments later we saw a puff of smoke followed seconds later by the tubing sound. The first round landed just outside the perimeter directly in front of us.

We scampered to grab a 60 mm mortar and some ammo. Danny put it between his legs without a tripod or a scope and began lobbing rounds in their direction while I fed him the ammo and stripped off the explosive increments. The next incoming mortar round landed well behind us.

The 106 mm recoilless rifle was positioned right next to us.

The operator turned the six-foot cannon 90 degrees on its tripod, chambered a round, and let go. As the final incoming mortar round came in, the NVA mortar emplacement across the ridge evaporated in a cloud of smoke, dust, and flesh.

Score one for the good guys.

The evening of June 4, 1968, our first night on LZ Loon, was relatively quiet. There was some probing of the lines, several grenades were thrown, and there was occasional small-arms fire.

All ours.

We heard the detonation of one claymore mine. Not a good sign. We slept—for the most part—stood regular watches, and sent out patrols and listening posts.

It was to be our last calm. One of the biggest battles of the Vietnam War was about to be joined.

By dawn of the third day, most of the marines of Charlie and Delta companies would be dead or wounded.

23

ON THE MORNING OF JUNE FIFTH, THE SUN ROSE TO inaugurate a spectacular spring day. But for the intense smell of cordite from the previous day's incoming mortars, the air was cool and fresh.

Several supply choppers came in early, bringing C rations, fresh fruit—unheard of in the field—pallets of ammo, and mail. We could hear the backhoe beginning to dig the 105 mm howitzer emplacements on the other side of our hill. As planned, the actual guns were to be dropped in by flying crane later in the morning. We would then commence our artillery assault on the encroaching enemy.

General Davis's plan was being implemented.

Our artillery would fire for two days and then be lifted out along with the rest of us to move on to another hill.

We all took a deep breath. Captain Negron, relieved by the absence of an incoming attack, sent out two squad-size patrols to look around just outside the lines for signs of enemy activity.

The patrols had neither NVA sightings nor contact, but did find an enemy canteen with blood trails nearby. The NVA had certainly been out there the night before. The morning passed uneventfully. We dug our holes deeper, cleaned our rifles, read our mail, and ate fresh fruit.

Early in the afternoon of June 5, choppers brought in Charlie Company's 3rd Platoon, which had been unable to land the previous day. Although we now had our full company, we were still severely undermanned. The promised replacement troops remained in the rear for the time being. An hour later, Lieutenant Colonel James MacLean, our battalion commander, accompanied by the artillery battalion commander, flew in by helicopter to inspect our emplacement. The two battalion commanders had been present with Alpha and Bravo companies during their heavy fighting the day before and they were concerned that we may have become vulnerable to a major NVA assault.

There was no question that we were dealing with hard-core NVA. In the southern regions of South Vietnam, a bad guy was called "Charlie." Here in the far northern reaches, we called him "Sir Charles."

He was worthy of our respect.

Alpha and Bravo companies had sustained four dead and twelve wounded from the attack on their nearby position the previous afternoon. For the first time since I'd arrived in country, all four companies of the 1st Battalion of the 4th Marine Regiment were in the shit at the same time.

Their mission accomplished, the two colonels boarded their helicopter. They had assured us that the promised artillery battery was on its way, would be dropped into place shortly, and would be ready to commence firing within the hour.

The artillery pieces never arrived.

With the colonels' helicopter still in plain view, the first deadly accurate incoming artillery and rockets from Co Roc, Laos, landed within our perimeter.

The battle for LZ Loon had commenced.

The cry of "Corpsman!" instantly rang out from near the 2nd Platoon's lines. There were injuries. This was serious. Several marines were wounded on the first round. The second round landed near an incoming supply chopper farther down the hill. Unharmed, it immediately lifted off and fled from the hill, but not before several off-loaded marines were injured. Terry Tillery received a pleading radio call from the 3rd Platoon radio operator, who, along with his platoon commander, Lieutenant Lloyd, had just jumped from the departing chopper.

"Charlie Six, this is Charlie Three. Over."

"Three, this is Six. Go," responded Tillery.

"Six, we got wounded down here. Lieutenant Lloyd is down. Looks like he got it in both legs. It's a fuckin' mess. Get some help down here. Now. Over."

"Roger, Three. Over and out."

Tillery released the handset, stood up, and yelled across the perimeter.

"We got wounded outside the lines that need help. Let's get down there. Come on."

Tillery ran down the hill, found Lieutenant Lloyd, and dragged him back up the hill. Several other marines scrambled down to guide the others up to safety.

While dealing with the incoming mortar and artillery fire, Negron kept an eye out on the horizon for the choppers with the artillery pieces. They never came. More alarming still, early that morning an army Huey helicopter had come in and removed the four engineers.

Great, thought Negron. *That's just fuckin' great. I've got two fuckin' pallets of howitzer ammo that will blow to kingdom come if they get hit with incoming artillery, and a huge fuckin' backhoe that the gooks will play target practice with. It has a full tank of gas, so it will probably blow as well.*

Just fuckin' great.

Like he didn't have enough on his mind already.

With sudden force, a deafening scream announced another incoming round. There had been no discernible muzzle blast. Like the other two, it came right at us and exploded with enormous force directly on top of a 2nd Platoon fighting hole. The cry went out for a corpsman, but the first corpsman to arrive saw no need. The hole, now four times its original size, contained an unidentifiable mélange of blood, hair, bones, and viscera.

We tried to remember who had been in the hole but were permitted little time to think.

The next round screamed in seconds later and landed in another hole on the 2nd Platoon lines. The force of both blasts was enormous and filled the air with the eerie sound of a million pieces of shrapnel fanning in all directions. We were being shelled with 122 mm artillery from Co Roc, Laos. This time, however, they had an excellent artillery forward observer. We had not heard such a sound since the previous December sixth, when the errant friendly bomb had landed on our position.

We cautiously emerged from our holes to look for confirmation that this had really happened. Instantly a third round came in. It whizzed inches over our heads, just missing the hill, and exploded with tremendous force in the valley below.

Danny Burton and I watched it in awe.

Even when we'd taken a direct hit on a bunker in Gio Linh, we had never heard such unbridled power or force. We snuck back into our holes and waited. The NVA had our complete and undivided attention. Charlie and Delta companies provided a big target on a small hill. The enemy had us in their sights.

We had nowhere to go.

We were pinned down.

The bombardment continued for more than an hour. Several more fighting holes were directly hit. Not a single subsequent round missed the hill. The cries of "Corpsman!" were unending.

The 2nd Platoon lines were particularly hard hit. Captain Negron passed the word for every available hand to get over there and start hauling the dead and wounded marines up to the LZ for evacuation.

I froze.

Was I an available hand?

I was not.

The ground attack would certainly come the second the last

round hit. The NVA knew when that would be. We didn't. I remained and kept a sharp eye out for NVA troop movement in the valley below. Like the others, I was a well-trained marine and well understood my role, even in the daunting chaos.

The next incoming round was their exclamation point.

It landed right on the LZ where the dead and wounded had been hauled. All of our available corpsmen were there treating the wounded, and all of our available volunteers were there attending to the bodies. The explosion was colossal. Dirt, shrapnel, and body parts flew by in all directions. Tiny pieces of searing metal lodged in my upper arms and shoulders outside of the protection of my flak jacket. I was completely covered with dirt.

Thanks to our training, though, we were able to again secure the LZ and, miraculously, get one last Marine Corps medevac chopper in. The three most severely wounded were slid aboard: 2nd Platoon machine gunner Wayne Wood, 2nd Platoon fire team leader Ric Popp, and my dear friend navy corpsman Mac Mecham.

Wood, from Cedar Rapids, Iowa, was so severely wounded that he would receive the last rites of the Catholic Church three times during the following week, but he would survive. Popp would recover from his wounds and later be returned to action. Mecham would lose his right thumb, which had been grotesquely mangled by shrapnel in the blast. He had been treating the wounded on the LZ.

As he boarded the outgoing helicopter, Mecham passed a handful of dog tags to one of the few corpsmen who remained.

"Here," he said. "Don't lose these."

With that, Mecham was hauled into the belly of the chopper, his legs dangling. The wheels lifted, the door gunner released a torrent of .50 caliber machine gun fire, and the bird banked off to the north and away.

The dog tags that Mecham handed off were those of each of the dead marines. He had been collecting them all day.

On our first morning on Parris Island, we were issued two dog tags. The first was to hang on a chain around our neck. The second was on a small chain hanging from the main chain. When a marine was killed, the second dog tag would be removed and kept with the unit for identification. The first remained on the body for final identification by the coroner in the rear.

Once the medevac was safely out, the corpsman delivered the pile of dog tags to Terry Tillery, rightfully assuming that they belonged with the command group.

"Here," he began, "somebody's got to be responsible for these because these guys are all dead." With that he dropped the muddy collection of stamped tin into Tillery's open palms.

Tillery wasn't sure what he was supposed to do with them, but he did know that they demanded his immediate attention. Slowly lowering himself back into the security of his fighting hole, he began the excruciating process of, one by one, carefully rubbing the dirt, mud, and blood off of each with his right thumb.

The dead came alive before his tearing eyes.

Carbaugh, W. F. Woody Carbaugh.

Carbaugh had replaced Tillery as a squad leader in the 2nd Platoon when Tillery had become a radio operator. He was from Thurmont, Maryland, not far from where Tillery's family had moved several years before. Barely twenty-one years old, Sergeant Carbaugh was dead. Tillery had thought that the first artillery round had landed near Carbaugh's hole. That was now confirmed. It had, in fact, landed inside of his small hole. Tillery unbuttoned the right thigh pocket of his pants and carefully placed Carbaugh's dog tag deep inside.

His right thumb then slowly rubbed over the surface of the second dog tag, removing the mud and the blood.

Klein, J. Joe Klein.

Tillery had noticed earlier that Klein and Carbaugh had been sharing a fighting hole. They must have died together, instantly. Joe Klein, a 2nd Platoon machine gunner from Highland Park, New Jersey, had just celebrated his nineteenth birthday. Tillery opened his pocket and carefully slid Joe Klein's dog tag inside.

Tillery was now becoming numb and disoriented. He still held a handful of dog tags.

Eaton, C. L.

Cliff Eaton from Cortland, New York, was a PFC grunt and another member of Tillery's and my former 2nd Platoon. He was twenty-one years old, and now dead.

Barbour, J. W.

Jim Barbour was a nineteen-year-old PFC from New Rochelle, New York.

Tillery was now in a fog. Tears rolled down his face, making it difficult to focus on the names as they appeared.

King, G. L., Jr.

George King, a nineteen-year-old PFC from Clatskanie, Oregon. King was a 2nd Platoon machine gunner. Tillery had last seen him, seconds before the final rocket, bravely hauling dead and wounded marines up the hill to the LZ under heavy incoming fire.

Morrissey, T. J., Jr.

Tom Morrissey. "Oh my God, no," said Tillery out loud. "Not Tom. Please not Tom." Morrissey, the yo-yo throwing, Ray-Ban shaded machine gunner, had been the soul of the 2nd Platoon. We all wanted to be like Tom—as a marine and as a person. He was the personification of a totally cool professional. He was a treasure, and now he was dead. Tom was married and had a young son, Tom the third, who was his pride and joy. He had barely seen the baby before he'd left for Vietnam from their home in Dover, New Hampshire. Corporal Tom Morrissey was five weeks shy of his twenty-first birthday.

Placing the rest of the dog tags in his pocket, Tillery took a deep breath, wiped his eyes, and crawled out of his hole to rejoin the Skipper.

The incoming artillery rounds were now walking their way back toward the Delta Company lines and away from us. Negron was desperately trying to get Marine Corps artillery and air support directed back to the guns in Co Roc. He was finally informed by John Camacho, his artillery forward observer, that our gunners were not permitted to fire on coordinates that were located inside of Laos.

"Fuck that shit," said Negron.

Negron pulled out his map and compass. He gave Camacho grid coordinates that were just inside the Vietnam border from Laos.

"Tell them to fire on these coordinates," said Negron. "After the first round, tell them to adjust outward on the next round. After the second round, tell them to adjust outward again on the third round."

Negron had been around. He knew that the artillery gunners had to report the requested grid coordinates but did not have to report on subsequent adjustments. With three of four adjustments, Camacho was able to move our artillery fire from safely within South Vietnam to directly on top of Co Roc, Laos.

Our defensive perimeter was now so thin that I could not see the manned holes on either side of me. Unless we did something fast, we'd be fucked—just as surely as if we were sitting in Khe Sanh or Con Thien. We were sitting ducks for their artillery, we were completely surrounded by a significantly superior force of ground troops, and night was falling. The guns had our coordinates perfectly. When dawn came, they'd begin again and finish us, assuming we survived the coming ground attack.

After dark, Negron hatched a plan.

Without telling battalion, he ordered those of us who remained to gather all of the ammo, ordnance, and water that we could carry and follow him across the ravine to the neighboring hill that was being tenuously held by Delta Company. He knew that the NVA had our precise coordinates on LZ Loon and that the barrage would, in all likelihood, begin again at dawn.

He hoped that by moving several hundred yards away from LZ Loon we could buy the necessary moments to evacuate the next morning before the NVA were able to recalibrate their guns onto the new position across the ravine.

Although many of the severely wounded had been evacuated, all of the dead marines remained on LZ Loon. Negron left Sergeant Brazier, half of the 3rd Platoon, and all of an 81 mm mortar squad to remain behind as a rear guard for the dead and the remaining ammo. Barring a nighttime ground assault, Negron hoped that he could get Brazier, his team, and the dead marines evacuated at first light the following morning before the artillery began anew. Negron also planned a brief return to LZ Loon the following morning to blow the backhoe and the pallet of artillery ammo that had been brought in the previous day.

Darkness fell. Exhausted, hungry, scared, and thirsty beyond all imagination, we grabbed every single item that we could carry and headed into the ravine. We were each loaded with more than a hundred pounds of ammo, mortars, .50 caliber machine guns, tripods, base plates, and as many mortar rounds as we could balance on top of everything else. Negron asked Lieutenant Jackson, the Delta Company commander, to send guides across to lead Charlie Company through the eye-high elephant grass. We silently plowed down the hill, crossed a small stream, and trudged up the other side. We set up our lines on the south side of the perimeter that faced back toward LZ Loon while Delta Company took their remaining marines to tighten the lines around the other side of the hill. Lieutenant Jackson met Negron upon arrival.

"Why'd you abandon the position?" Jackson whispered in a barely audible voice.

Negron replied, "I have a feeling that this whole fuckin' area is going to turn to shit real soon."

There was no way that Jackson, or anyone else for that matter, could disagree with the decision.

We silently moved around our side of the new perimeter, found our holes, set up lines of fire, and armed the claymore mines in front of us. We sent out neither ambushes nor listening posts. Nor did we establish watch schedules. There would be no sleep for Charlie Company tonight. We did, however, say our prayers.

All night long, we heard the movement of NVA soldiers just outside the lines, with the squeak of their gear and the soft snap of an occasional stick. We heard the snipers climb up into the trees and even heard whispers.

It was eerie and scary beyond all imagination.

Once all of the necessary tasks were completed, there was nothing to do but collapse into our holes and wait. We knew where they were, and they knew where we were.

24

IT BECAME APPARENT WITH THE EARLIEST LIGHT OF dawn that the NVA plan had been to wear us down with the artillery attack the previous day and assault us with ground troops that morning. We knew they were in place; we'd been listening to them all night. Although short on ammo and manpower, we were ready too.

Neither side could now make a move without its registering on the other.

It was time.

The uneasy silence was broken with a roar of rifle fire. At first, all of the shots were from the distinctive-sounding Russian-built AK-47s that were the weapon of choice for the North Vietnamese Army. An instant later, we heard some light returning fire from the American M16 rifles. It was over in less than a minute, and then there was no sound at all. The shots had been coming from the direction of the ravine between the two hills—the same ravine that we had crossed the previous evening on our way to our current position. We were unable to see a thing, but we quickly assumed that the return fire must have been from Sergeant Brazier's squad that had been left behind to guard LZ

Loon. They were the only marines outside of our lines. At once
Tillery's radio crackled.

"Charlie Six, this is Charlie Three. Over." Tillery recognized
the voice of Eddie Mitchell, the 3rd Platoon radio operator.

"Go ahead, Three," Tillery responded.

"Six," Mitchell was yelling into his handset. "Six, Brazier's
down, he's dead. It's a fuckin' mess. We're headed back over to
LZ Loon. Over and out."

At daybreak, Sergeant Brazier had begun to lead his squad
over to our new hill from LZ Loon. The dead had been gathered
and prepared for later evacuation, and the explosive charges had
been set on the backhoe and the ammo pallet. At the base of the
ravine between the two adjacent hills, Brazier's squad of marines
had walked right into a well-set NVA ambush. Brazier, walking
point, had never had a chance. He was instantly killed with five
rounds into his chest. Dragging their leader behind, the rest of
the squad beat a hasty retreat back to the tenuous safety of LZ
Loon and dug back in.

Seconds after Mitchell's radio transmission, all hell broke
loose.

The AK-47 fire began coming from every point around the
perimeter. Several bullets exploded inches over my helmet; others whizzed past my ears. Marines are fond of saying that you
never hear the one that hits you. In that I took some comfort. As
long as I could hear the crack of the rounds on their way by, I
knew that I was still alive. The rifle fire was followed in succes-
sion by rocket-propelled grenades and mortars.

There was no place to hide.

The NVA were everywhere.

"Grasshopper Charlie Six, this is Grasshopper Six Actual.
Things sound kinda rough up there for you. Give me a sit rep.
Over." Lieutenant Colonel James MacLean, our visitor from the
previous day, was on the radio checking in.

"Grasshopper Six, this is Charlie Six Actual. We are in the
V ring. Surrounded by unhappy gooks. Send water, ammo, air,

and arty. *Now.* Over." Bill Negron was totally focused on our immediate survival.

"Charlie Six, this is Grasshopper Six. I read you loud and clear. What's your body count? Over."

"Grasshopper Six, be advised that I've lost an entire offensive football team and one baseball team. I'm too busy killing 'em to count 'em. I'll be back when it's quieter. Over." Negron signed off.

"Roger that, Charlie Six. Groceries and goodies are on the way. Over and out."

A brief radio silence was followed by an urgent whisper on another radio that was barely audible.

"Charlie Six, this is Charlie Three. Over."

It was the voice of 3rd Platoon radio operator Mitchell calling again from LZ Loon across the ravine.

"This is Six. Go," replied Tillery.

"Six, they're coming at you. We can see it from here. They're all over your fuckin' perimeter and they are coming at you. Over."

Negron grabbed the handset from Tillery.

"Three, this is Six Actual, do you read me? Over."

"Roger that, Skipper." Mitchell was out of breath and scared.

"Three, can you give me their grid coordinates. Give me some numbers so I can lay some lumber on them."

With that, two more 122 mm rockets screamed over the perimeter, followed by a volley of incoming grenades, mortars, and small-arms fire. The ground attack had begun.

"Here they come!" someone screamed.

"Gooks in the perimeter!" came the cry from the 2nd Platoon lines.

"Gooks in the perimeter!" came the cry again, now from the Delta Company lines. Delta marines were engaged in hand-to-hand combat with the enemy.

Negron, observing the assault, looked calmly to John Camacho, the artillery forward observer, and gave a sullen nod.

"Do it. Do it now."

Camacho picked up his handset and called the rear. Negron then turned to Terry Tillery and said, "Pass the word. Get everybody in a hole. *Now.*"

"All stations on this net, this is Charlie Six," Tillery advised. "Be advised we are calling them in on us. Repeat, calling them in on us. Pass the word. Get down. Now. Over."

Negron, Camacho, and Tillery slid into a small command bunker they'd dug out the night before. Had there been time, they'd have dug it a mile deeper.

Minutes passed.

Camacho got final confirmation of the coming artillery bombardment from the rear and, eschewing the radio, yelled "ON THE WAY!" and leapt back into the bunker. Around the perimeter, from hole to hole, came the cries of "ON THE WAY!" and "FIRE IN THE HOLE!" At once, we all got small.

Camacho, on Negron's order, had instructed our supporting artillery to fire directly onto our position, and we prayed like hell that none of the rounds fell directly into any of our fighting holes. We had little choice. The NVA had broken through our lines in several places and were now inside our perimeter.

The following seconds passed in near silence but for the sporadic crack of an AK-47 rifle. Then it came. The air at once was filled with exploding artillery, flying shrapnel, and screaming boys.

Their boys.

The artillery air bursts, ordered by Camacho, had caught the enemy in the open. Instead of exploding on impact, the artillery had been fused to ignite in the air above the battlefield. It was a slaughter.

With the last explosion, we leapt from the safety of our holes to reinforce the lines and ensure that every NVA soldier who had penetrated the perimeter was dead.

They were scattered everywhere, and they were all very dead. June 6, 1968.

It had felt like a lifetime, and the morning was only half over.

Since the opening assault on Sergeant Brazier's squad at dawn, we had lost twenty-seven men. Three of our four hospital corpsmen were wounded, and, except for Negron, we were out of officers—all were dead or wounded. We were tired, thirsty, scared, and trapped. We were low on ammo, water, and men. There were perhaps eighty of us left out of the one hundred eighty who had made the original landing, trying desperately to man an ever shrinking perimeter.

Our ammo supply was of particular concern. We were running out of what little we had been able to take with us from LZ Loon the night before. What we did have was being rationed around the lines. Frank McCormack, who had joined us just as we'd left Camp Carroll, occupied himself by identifying who had ammo and who needed it and running around the lines constantly passing it out or picking it up. He would later receive a Bronze Star for his efforts that day. A resupply chopper that had been able to get in around midmorning had been shot down on takeoff and had crashed on the side of the hill. Several of us ran up to retrieve the valuable cargo from the hulking shell, bringing cases and cases of 7.62 mm machine gun ammo, .223 caliber rifle shells, and 60 mm mortar rounds back down to the fight.

"Skipper." It was radio operator Tillery. "There's a Trailblazer Six Actual on the battalion TAC-NET."

"Who the fuck is Trailblazer Six?" Negron wanted to know. "For shit's sake, Tillery, can't you keep even a few of these assholes off the line until we figure out how in the fuck we're going to get out of this?" Negron was becoming uncharacteristically frustrated. "Jesus Christ, we got enough fuckin' 'Sixes' clogging up this motherfuckin' line."

Negron grabbed the extended handset, took a quick breath, and squeezed the handle. "This is Charlie Six Actual. Over."

"Charlie Six Actual, this is Trailblazer Six Actual. I know it's hot up there; I know you're in the shit. I know you think I'm another rear jockey pain in the ass, but we gotta get you all out of there and soon, so give me a sit rep."

"Trailblazer Six Actual, the bad guys are still here. We're dug in and kicking ass. You want my opinion? Get us out of here and bomb the shit out of it. Over."

"Roger that, Charlie Six. I read you. Hold on to what you've got. Help is on the way. Over and out."

On the way, my ass, thought Negron. And who in the hell was Trailblazer Six Actual, anyway?

Within minutes, a CH-46 helicopter and a protecting Huey gunship appeared on the horizon and banked toward LZ Loon across the ravine. We were ordered to lay down as much fire as we could in that direction but to avoid the LZ where Sergeant Brazier's former squad and the 81 mm mortar squad were mustering for evacuation. The CH-46 banked in quickly and hovered just above the ground while the thirteen marines quickly climbed in.

We kept up our covering fire, at once relieved and wistful to see *them* getting evacuated, and filled with hope that perhaps we would be next. At least we knew that we had someone's attention in the rear.

Our eyes were fixated on the chopper as it lifted and banked, but it didn't seem able to gain altitude. We began to cheer for it.

"Come on. Get up, get up, get *up*."

But it was not able to elevate.

It had been shot.

It was going down.

It had reached the edge of the far side of the hill, but we watched in horror as the mortally wounded helicopter hit the treetops, began to roll, and then disappeared from sight. Seconds later the explosion came. There was smoke, and then there was silence. Incredibly and unbelievably, we were informed by a spotter plane a short time later that they had seen at least two survivors.

One of the survivors was Corporal Sal Santangelo from Brooklyn.

It had already been a horrifying two days for Santangelo. The day before, while we were under ground attack, he'd felt something hit the front of his helmet. Afraid of what he'd find, he moved his right hand up to feel the spot. There was a small hole the size of the end of his index finger.

"Sal," cried his hole mate, inches away. "Sal, you've been shot."

Santangelo feared that he must be dying and waited for the life to drain out of him. Seconds later, gathering his nerve, he ran his hand around the back of the helmet to find a much larger exit hole.

Now he was certain that he was dead.

Slowly bending down and taking off his helmet, he looked at the two aligned holes—front to back. Then he took his hand and slowly rubbed is scalp. It was still there. The bullet had gone right through without touching him.

He was alive.

Now Santangelo had a bigger problem.

Having been thrown from the chopper on impact with one other marine that he could see, he was down in the jungle with a smashed right leg, well outside of our lines, and in all likelihood living the last moments of his life. When later asked what he did, he said, "I held my breath for as long as I could, trying to kill myself. That didn't work out too well, so I crawled over to this other guy who was in pretty bad shape to see if we could figure something out."

Two marines together can always figure something out.

Those of us from Charlie and Delta companies that remained on the hill could now hear the sound of the approaching jet fighters.

"On the way!" came the now familiar cry. Those who were exposed ran back into their holes. The first pass brought two Phantoms. What a sight. They passed, one after the other, no more than fifty yards in front of my position. It was the most awesome display of raw power I had ever seen. Behind the deafening roar, I could hear the cracks of AK-47 rifle fire from the ravine directly beneath the planes. The dumb-ass gooks, facing certain death, were firing up at the jets.

You couldn't blame them for trying. That day alone, the

NVA had shot down two CH-46 helicopters, the one fully loaded with marines being evacuated, and the other with desperately needed ammo and water.

Negron, watching the awesome spectacle, quietly wondered again about the identity of Trailblazer Six. Whoever he was, it was clear that we finally had the attention of someone in authority.

The two jets, back at full altitude, took a long turn from the south, banked east, headed north, and banked west to south to commence another run. Minutes later, down they came again at the same target, with me yards away watching in awed appreciation. Shortly before reaching its low point on this pass, the lead jet released two oblong silver canisters one after the other. The canisters tumbled forward and down.

Hoooleee shit. Napalm.

I watched with horror and disbelief. My face was frozen to the target as the canisters hit the treetops, opened, and exploded, making my face and eyebrows instantly hot with the torrent of otherworldly flame. The sound was that of an eerie *whooossshhh* as the jellied wall of flame, heat, and horror consumed and sucked oxygen from all that was in, and tunneled below, its path. There were some screams, but muffled.

The second Phantom followed on an identical run. No AK-47s were heard. I put my head down as the second payload of canisters was dropped, and listened for the screams.

There were none.

The target had been annihilated.

The fighting continued sporadically for the rest of the afternoon. The two remaining corpsmen had their hands full as they crawled from one wounded marine to another to stop the bleeding and administer immediate triage. One corpsman was working fruitlessly on Mel Langston, a nineteen-year-old private first class from Valentine, Nebraska. Langston had been shot through the helmet and had a bullet lodged in his skull. The round was clearly visible in his head. He died an hour later.

The sky remained filled with rocket-laden Huey gunships

that were making regular assaults on the enemy positions. High above, there was a spotter plane directing fire, but the NVA kept coming. We continued to take wounded and continued to contract our perimeter up the hill to compensate for the increasing manpower shortage.

As the afternoon wore on, Bill Negron was becoming concerned about the two reported helicopter crash survivors that were out there somewhere. They were probably lost, certainly disoriented, and would have no way, in all the confusion, of knowing where we were.

So, he hatched another plan.

Gathering most of us who were on that side of the hill, he had us stand in loose formation and, with every ounce of breath that we could muster, sing "The Marines' Hymn."

From the Halls of Montezuma,
To the Shores of Tripoli;
We fight our country's battles
In the air, on land, and sea . . .

I am not kidding.

At the time, I thought that we were just giving a big fuck-you to the enemy, but the Skipper would never have needlessly put us in harm's way. Instead, he was trying to signal to the two lost marines so that they would know where we were.

Minutes later, the familiar sound of rotors rose behind us as two marine helicopters flew over to survey the crash site for survivors. The sound of the AK-47 fire directed at them again became deafening. The pilot spotted several hundred uniformed NVA soldiers several hundred meters east of the downed chopper. Incredibly, over the next twenty minutes, with covering fire from the air and the ground, the rescue chopper was able to extract Corporal Santangelo and three other marines—two had been part of the downed chopper's crew.

Given the crash of the two helicopters and the near-impossible evacuation that he had just witnessed, Bill Negron knew now that our chances of being evacuated were remote at best. He could barely imagine that even a marine helicopter pilot would take such a suicidal risk. We were surrounded by a vastly superior force and were low on ammo. Nightfall was coming.

Negron needed a new plan.

If we stayed on the hill, we would in all likelihood die.

It would be one hell of a fight, and we would take legions of them with us, but losing the balance of an entire Marine Corps rifle company was not an option. He passed the word that we should gather every compass and map that we could find. We had already taken all of the serviceable equipment from the dead. Any of the wounded who had been evacuated had left their compasses, maps, water, and ammo behind.

We were in better shape than Negron might have thought. There were maps and compasses for nearly every marine who was left.

Negron then passed the word that we would most likely be leaving by foot shortly after dark. We would be in three-man teams, quietly abandon the hill, and head due north through the jungle using our escape and evasion training and skills.

Several miles due north was Route 9. It was open and secure during daylight hours. All we had to do was keep heading due north all night. Some of us would make it; most of us probably would not. That being said, we would all live or die like marines—on the offensive. No question that we would take out a mess of gooks along the way.

If we stayed, we would die.

If we left, we had a chance.

We gathered our gear.

I was scared, but well understood that it was our only chance. Compass reading had not been my strong suit, but even I could follow a north-facing arrow. As our moment grew closer, I became increasingly excited. We'd been defensive sitting ducks for almost three days. If I was going to die, as seemed likely, I wanted to be on the attack like the United States Marine that I was.

All felt as I did.

Fuck 'em.

Fuck 'em all.

We were going to take as many of those little motherfuckers down with us as we could.

The moment never came.

Within the hour, several helicopters, against all odds and through heavy ground fire, came in and began to pull us out. It was a dream. As each successive chopper loaded, we shrank the perimeter and moved uphill. I was on the third chopper out. I ran for the raising ramp and was pulled in by as many hands as were already on the helicopter. We lifted, banked, and heard small-arms fire ding off the chopper's belly. The two .50 caliber door gunners at once laid down a massive wall of suppressive fire. Minutes later when we saw the craters of Khe Sanh outside the shattered windows, we knew that we were safe for the first time in three days.

As there had been no formal plan for our evacuation, the pilots off-loaded us to several of the secured rear bases along Route 9. Most of us ended up at the Vandergrift Combat Base. In the two-hundred-year history of the U.S. Marine Corps, there was not a single marine who felt more tested and battle hardened than we did that evening.

Captain Negron, last to disembark, directed our staggering beleaguered lot to a nearby mess tent where hot chow and water were in abundance. We mustered forward in dazed disbelief, hugging, touching, crying, and looking about for friends, knowing that more than a few remained on the hill.

Dead.

Then a voice came from behind.

"Charlie Six Actual, I presume?"

Negron snapped around to see a familiar-looking stranger walking slowly toward him across the tarmac, arm and hand outstretched. "Good job, Captain. I'm proud of you and proud of your company.

"Trailblazer here. Trailblazer Six Actual."

Only then did Negron recognize the familiar face. It was that of Raymond G. Davis, the new commanding general of the entire 3rd Marine Division. During those final hours, the besieged boys of Charlie Company were given the full attention and resources of the entire 3rd Division of the United States Marine Corps.

For those three days in June 1968, Charlie and Delta companies 1/4 *were* the war in Vietnam.

25

THE NEXT MORNING WE BEGAN TO GATHER UP THE
disparate elements of Charlie Company that had been evacuated
from LZ Loon to various bases along Route 9. Captain Negron
decided that we would consolidate there at the Vandergrift
Combat Base, so one by one throughout the morning, we were
reunited with our lost comrades. Each person carried a valuable
piece of information about the casualties. These guys were at
Delta Med in Dong Ha, some other guys were in Da Nang. A
bunch, including Wayne Wood and Michael Kilderry, were on
the hospital ship *Repose* offshore. And, finally, all these guys—
the long list that we were soon all able to recite by rote—were
dead.

All dead.

There were fresh tears, breathless reunions, and the early
telling and retelling of the hundreds of stories that emerged from
the three-day battle. We had to keep talking to one another to be
certain it had not been a nightmare.

"How did you make it out?"

"Did Santangelo make it back?"

"What happened to the pilot of the ammo chopper that got
shot down?"

"How bad was Doc Mac hurt? Did anyone see where he got hit?"

"What's Snowball doing on the *Repose*; it didn't look like he got hit too bad."

"Is Woody still alive? It didn't look like there was anything left of him when we threw him on the chopper."

And so it went, all day and through the night, and into the next day. Fragments of information came in, and rumors abounded. What we all knew to be true was that of our already understaffed company of one hundred eighty marines who'd landed on LZ Loon, only sixty of us came off the hill in the end. At least twenty-two of the dead were left behind. That was the nightmarish reality for all of us. We had left them there. We desperately wanted to go right back to LZ Loon and get them, but it was not to be for at least another week.

We were all confident that it would be a long time before we got sent back into the shit. It would take weeks to reman the company and weeks more to bring the new guys up to speed. There was talk of a "float phase." Occasionally, undermanned companies such as ours were sent onto ships offshore to regroup, practice amphibious landings, and, of particular interest to us, get leave in the squalid Philippine liberty port of Olongapo. I figured that I had about six weeks left in the field before going home. I was safe. The war was over for me.

Soon enough, new guys poured in, all as green as grass. They looked at us as though we'd just stepped out of some war movie. Their eyes were as big as globes as they heard us recount our stories. Some were scared; most were pissed that they had missed the action. As had become his custom, Bill Negron took each one aside, welcomed him, and passed on his wisdom of the ages.

"This is serious business," he'd begin. "When your squad leader tells you to do something, do it. Move on command. Don't ask questions. Am I making myself clear?"

"Yes, sir," would come the obedient reply.

"I'm not 'sir' out here, son. I'm Bill or I'm Skipper. Gooks hear someone call me sir, I'm a dead man. Get it?" Negron was always clear about this.

"Yes . . . ah . . . Skipper," would come the uncertain reply.

"Good man. Good man. Look, you want to stay alive, listen to the old guys, the veterans who've been in the shit. They'll get you through it."

This would be followed by a warm arm on the shoulder and an encouraging word. "You're going to be fine, Marine."

With that, Negron would call Tillery and have him escort the new guy to his assigned platoon, squad, and fire team.

"Tillery," he'd call.

The radio man would obediently run right over.

"Sir. Yes, sir?" Tillery couldn't resist. He loved to give the Skipper shit.

And Negron would laugh.

"Get this marine over to 2nd Platoon on the double."

Bill Negron could be an intimidating person when you first met him. He was as tough as nails, had a big brown square jaw, and appeared wired to blow—he was that intense. But he also was as personable and as nice a man as any of us had ever met.

He cared.

He talked to his men.

He never pulled a punch. He taught us everything he knew—and he knew a lot.

He was the best.

The fresh marines brought one piece of news from home that felt like the last straw. Bobby Kennedy, New York senator Robert F. Kennedy, Jr., brother of the slain President John F. Kennedy, candidate for the presidency of the United States, had been killed days before, while we were on LZ Loon.

What the fuck was going on back home? Jesus.

Our days of comfort were short-lived. We were ordered to saddle up with full packs, helmets, and flak jackets. We were issued chow, water, and fresh ammo.

The choppers came and we headed back out into the shit.

Consistent with Ray Davis's new policy, we were choppered

into LZ Robin. Like LZ Loon, it too was hard on the Laotian border. The artillery was already in place this time. It was an impressive battery of 105 mm howitzers—what might have been at LZ Loon had we gotten them in. Alpha Company was already in place as well and showed no signs of departing. Temporarily homeless, we took our small band of marines and climbed all the way down the hill and all the way up the next one. We dug out holes. If some were already there, we dug them deeper.

For the following three days, until Alpha vacated, we occupied a small perimeter that we dubbed Robin Alpha. It was too small for a helicopter landing, so every morning we'd send a working party back over to Alpha to pick up mail, fresh ammo, and C rations. It was a haul and we hated it. This was a long way from the nightlife in Olongapo we had dreamed of.

On the second morning, we discovered an enemy tunnel inside the perimeter. It was not uncommon to find one, but the fact that it was inside our lines grabbed our immediate attention. It was said that an NVA soldier could go from the Ho Chi Minh Trail in Laos to Saigon and never see the light of day. This may have been an exaggeration, but perhaps not. The tunnel complex directly under LZ Loon that had been pointed out to me by Leeland Johnson upon my arrival on June 4 was later found to include a barracks and a medical station.

As was customary, one of the smallest marines was asked to volunteer for the task of going into the tunnel—to be the tunnel rat. I was six feet, three inches tall, though very skinny. Any time that tunnel rat volunteers were called for, I'd stand as tall as I was able and puff out my chest. Days before on LZ Loon, I'd provided the largest target there was to the enemy, and there wasn't a second that I didn't curse my parents for passing on the big-person gene. At this moment, though, I was a giant and did all that I could to see that everyone noticed. I had no interest in being a tunnel rat.

The volunteer was picked, and, after having a rifle sling tied around his leg, he was lowered into the abyss. It's hard to describe how small the hole was or to imagine how any person could get in. Moments passed with little sound but some movement that we could detect. Those of us not on watch gathered closely around. Then, for several minutes, there was nothing.

A second marine, Dwayne Slate, who only weeks earlier had procured all of our new combat gear, was sent down. He spotted the first marine on the bottom, dead. We were never told his cause of death but assumed that it was from the lack of air in the tunnel.

Slate couldn't breathe, so we pulled him up before he died.

It was an excruciating moment for all of us.

We had just suffered another casualty, and for what?

Some time later, a diminutive major from Alpha Company came over and, armed with ropes and appropriate gear, went back down into the hole and retrieved the dead, dirty, ashen-faced marine.

It was a numbly horrifying moment.

The poor fuck had survived LZ Loon and died in this little shit hole.

Bill Negron was distraught. An hour later, after it had sunk in, we saw him quietly crying with his head held in his hands.

It was an awful moment, a terrifyingly helpless moment.

That afternoon, a chaplain was sent out. It had originally been planned as a time of remembrance for the boys lost on LZ Loon, but the recent tragedy gave it new overtones. We all stood silently on the inside lip of a bomb crater with our heads bowed and listened to his comforting words. He led us in prayer. He handed out rosary beads and crosses to all who wanted them. I had never seen rosary beads before, but in the event that they might have some value, I kept them in my pocket for the balance of my tour. How could it hurt?

Later in the week, we went on a small operation about a thousand meters to the west. Walking through the tall grass and dense bush, the point man suddenly found himself face-to-face with two NVA soldiers. His M16 at the ready, he shot and killed them both before either could react. Our nerves, already shot, sparked with the first sound of rifle fire since LZ Loon. We scouted the area, and determined that the two enemy troops were alone. Negron then called up to the point man and asked that the two bodies be brought to the perimeter that we were forming for the evening. Propping the bodies up next to a tree, he called the new replacements over for a quick lesson.

"Can you all see this? Come on, gather around closer and let me see a tight circle. Okay. You all see this now? This is what happens out here. This is serious business."

Several new marines broke ranks and began to throw up. "You are all going to be here for thirteen months, if you are lucky. You will sleep outside every night. Most of your meals will come out of a can. The enemy will be watching you constantly. . . . Constantly. Do you all understand that?"

Silence.

"You never really believe what's going to happen till it happens to you. Then you say, 'Oh, shit, I better really pay attention now.' Well, this is it. You don't pay attention, you end up like this." Negron rubbed the dead NVA soldier on the head for emphasis. "Ten minutes ago, this poor fuck was alive and thinkin' about pussy and beer, just like you. This will be you if you don't do what you are told and listen to your leaders.

"Thank you, men. You're dismissed."

We old guys were too numb to notice. Most of the new guys were sick with fear.

Eleven days after LZ Loon, on June 17, we got the word that we had been waiting for. The Skipper was looking for volunteers to go back to LZ Loon to retrieve our dead marines. To a man, we all wanted to go and begged that he leave no one behind. Those were our brothers back there. We also were silently hoping that we might get a little payback in the process.

The following morning, we saddled up with helmets, flak jackets, and gas masks. There would be a terrible stench, not only from our dead comrades but from what we could only imagine to be hundreds of rotting napalmed NVA soldiers. We were given Compazine to be certain that our stomachs stayed settled. Our mission was to get in, get the bodies, and get out.

One platoon was to go down to the site of the helicopter crash, while the other two platoons were to canvass the hill. In addition to our normal ammo and gear, we carried body bags and grappling hooks, in the event that the bodies had been booby-trapped with hand grenades. The 2nd Battalion, 9th Marines came in right behind us and set up perimeter security to protect us while we executed our morbid mission.

The operation went off without a hitch. The choppers dropped us off under a heavy layer of smoke that had been dropped as a shield for protection from the Co Roc guns. We wanted to make it impossible for the forward observer to re-create his deadly bearings. Given the nature of the mission, we were accompanied by the press for the first and only time during my tour. A photograph of the mission appeared on the front page of *The New York Times* days later. It showed four of us carrying the bagged remains of the crashed helicopter pilot past a staked American flag that we found in Tom Morrissey's pocket. He always carried it with him.

The dead bodies that we had left behind on the night of June 5 when we'd moved to the other hill were still on the LZ exactly as they had been left. We silently began the task of identifying them, bagging them, and preparing them for evacuation. We also found Sergeant Brazier's body and several of the others who had been killed during the third day of the battle. Dan Burton was called over to make the identifications, as he was one of the few marines left from the decimated 2nd Platoon. It was the hardest thing he ever had to do. Morrissey's mostly dismembered body, a trigger for Dan's nightmares since, was the most frightening figure imaginable, bearing the otherworldly facial expression with which he left this earth. Only four of the other bodies were identifiable to the eye.

The enemy bodies were everywhere.

There were hundreds of them, and they all appeared young and small.

It was obvious that the NVA too had left in a hurry; they generally were as meticulous as we in removing their dead. Most of the bodies that I saw were burned on one part or another from the napalm. I softly kicked the helmet of one of the NVA dead and removed most of his rotting scalp in the process.

It was ghastly.

Mission completed, I began to head back to the LZ with the rest of my squad to prepare for evacuation. On the dusty narrow path, my eye caught sight of what appeared to be a cigar. How peculiar, I thought. A cigar. Do they smoke cigars? I was puzzled, so I reached down and picked it up. Now standing and holding the object, I realized with revulsion that it was in fact a human thumb. I let it fall back to the path. For years this was a source of my own nightmares. By then, I had been informed that Doc Mac Mecham had lost his thumb in the battle. Thirty-eight years later when I finally found Doc Mac, it was one of the first questions I asked him.

"Doc," I began. "Doc, you lost your thumb during the rocket attack on LZ Loon."

"Right," came the simple response, wondering where I was going with this.

"Doc, did you, like, lose it right there, or did they take it off later?"

"No. In the rear. They took it off in Dong Ha, I think. The hand was a mess, but they couldn't save the thumb. Why do you ask?"

"No reason," I quietly responded. "No reason. I'm just glad you're alive."

"No shit, Jack. Me too."

And so the conversation ended.

The choppers came back a few minutes later, and, with little fanfare, we loaded the body bags, boarded, and headed three minutes back to LZ Robin. Looking down, it was not lost on me that the last time we had all been together in the air, the five dead boys at my feet had been sitting across the aisle ready to go into battle, not prone on the deck ready to go home. We were fortunate. Although we wouldn't know how fortunate until the following morning. The 2nd Battalion, 9th Marines, which had been holding lines while we retrieved the bodies, began getting hit with the artillery from Co Roc as soon as we left. They took twelve incoming rounds and a number of casualties before they too were able to get evacuated.

My head was pounding by the time we got back to Robin. The smell—the rotting flesh, the cordite, the sulfur—was all too much to endure. Our hands and clothes were covered with the blood and innards of the bodies. Wipe your nose once, and the smell would stay for days. The only water on Robin Alpha was in our canteens. We tried to wash the stink off, but it was impossible. Throughout the balance of the afternoon, marines would find quiet spots just outside the lines and vomit.

We were tired—exhausted. Our nerves were like crystal and we stank to high heaven. Bill Negron did his best to keep our morale up, but it was a near-impossible challenge. The rumors of a float phase continued, as did rumors of just going back to Dong Ha for a few weeks to regroup. The season had instantly changed to summer and it was now unbearably hot. Our daily bath consisted of removing our olive T-shirt, wiping the sweat from our bodies, and putting it back on. Sweaty as we were, it was an effective way to get the dirt off. We had worn the same boots, pants, T-shirts, and socks since we'd left the Washout three weeks earlier.

The following morning we watched with unbridled joy as Alpha Company was lifted off of LZ Robin. We gathered our gear and headed down into the ravine and back up the hill for the last time to take over the lines. It was heaven. No more walking back and forth for supplies, and there was a large water tank that was the next best thing to a hot bath, as far as we were concerned. The only downside was that it was noisy. The big 105 mm howitzers fired all day and all night long, shaking the ground and splitting our ears. The hilltop was so small that there was no place to get away from them.

For the next seven days, we manned our lines, ate our C rations, read our daily mail, cleaned our rifles, and sent out patrols during the day and ambushes and listening posts during the night. We'd make occasional contact, but we were becoming increasingly numb to the NVA presence. We were just doing our jobs and watching out for one another.

Some big brass flew in one day, including General Henry W. Buse, the new commanding general of the Fleet Marine Force, Pacific (FMFPac), which meant he was in charge of all marines in the Pacific (including us). His headquarters were in Hawaii, so he was a long way from home. He awarded several well-deserved Bronze Stars for action on LZ Loon.

We later joked that he probably got a Silver Star just for coming out to our little hill.

We left Robin about a week later, abandoning the position. We set fire to and blew up all that was in our wake so as not to leave the enemy even a C ration can. We returned to Vandergrift to regroup, take showers, get clean clothes, and pick up more replacement troops.

By the end of June, freed from the chains of partisan politics, President Johnson admitted that it would be impossible for the United States to pay for both "guns and butter." On June 28, he signed into law a bill that called for both a 10 percent income tax surcharge and significant reductions in government spending. The fiscal strain on Washington to pay for Johnson's Great Society programs while financing an increasingly costly war half a world away was beginning to catch up with the extraordinary human sacrifice.

By Wednesday, July 3, 1968, news of our three days at LZ Loon and the ensuing body snatch had reached an increasing number of press outlets in the United States. The *San Diego Evening Tribune* featured a front-page article titled "Marines Always Pay Their Debt to Dead." It contained a photograph of a very tough-looking Bill Negron with the quote "I personally wouldn't want live Marines coming in for me if I were killed out there. But I know their parents, their wives and sweethearts would. We have an obligation to them."

....

During the first week of July, I got word that my flight date out of country had been assigned. I would be leaving from Da Nang on July 30, 1968. Those rotating home normally left the field ten days before departure, which meant I had just less than three weeks left.

The following days were spent doing what combat marines in Vietnam did. We boarded helicopters, opened new firebases, or took over ones that were there. We ran patrols, sweltered in the sun, engaged in the occasional small firefight, and always returned to Vandergrift for a night to get resupplied. The following morning we'd be off again. Perhaps road security this time, or a company-size patrol into the bush. It was hard, grueling work, but we all seemed to thrive on the routine and enjoyed the activity. Bill Negron was now an integral part of our lives, and we were deeply happy for that. We would do whatever he told us to do because we always knew that he would be the first to go in and the last to come out.

Every time.

....

The morning of my departure from the field was bittersweet. I had said my good-byes earlier and now sat to the side of the LZ waiting for the supply chopper to come in and take me to Dong Ha, the first leg on my journey home.

The marines of Charlie Company had spent the morning in high activity in preparation for another operation to the west. They were now positioned across the small LZ from where I sat with all of my gear. Since Charlie Company was headed off on an operation for an indeterminate time, Captain Negron let me go a few days early to be certain that I made my flight out from Da Nang the following week.

It was odd—eerie—watching my Charlie Company saddle up without me with their full packs and ammo, as we had done so many times before. There were some hugs and a few waves, but the boys were headed back off into the shit. There was work to be done. I could visualize the scene inside the chopper. When they became airborne, squeezed along the bulkhead with the weight of the world on their backs, they'd look at the man across the aisle and share a thumbs-up. On our way, we never sweated anything. It was a wonderful quality of being a marine. A can-do attitude permeated all that we did. I would miss it. I would never again share that kind of a bond with anyone. The chopper would land, and they'd charge off and hit the deck as far from the helicopter as they could get.

The daily mail chopper came in minutes later. I hitched a ride on it back to Dong Ha. I was no longer a member of Charlie Company. Within days, I would no longer be a United States Marine.

I was so very sad.

I was so very happy.

Mostly, I felt very alone.

26

MY FINAL DAYS IN VIETNAM WERE SPENT IN DA NANG, waiting for my flight home while trying to wangle out of getting the required gamma globulin shot. Every marine beginning and ending a Vietnam tour was required to have one. Back stateside, we used to hear that it took three men to carry the needle. Before I left Okinawa on my way over, I realized that this was not much of an exaggeration. I hated needles, although I had come to love navy corpsmen. It was a conundrum until, hours before my flight, a doc approached and said, "The needle, Corporal McLean, or back to the field."

I never felt a thing.

Home in New England, the Newport Folk Festival was in full swing. The launching pad for Joan Baez and Bob Dylan years before was now featuring the young son of American folk icon Woody Guthrie. Arlo Guthrie seemed a whiny cross between his father and Bob Dylan, although he *could* play the guitar and he had a gift for storytelling—*long* storytelling. On July 24, 1968, he debuted his twenty-minute ballad "Alice's Restaurant" to rave reviews.

"Alice's Restaurant" is a song about dodging the draft and the ridiculously humorous lengths to which someone might go to do so. To many boys of that generation, however, no length was too ridiculous. The draft was a deadly serious sword of Damocles that hung over the head of every healthy boy in America.

I, however, was on my way home.

Shortly I would become the only person I knew, or that anyone that I knew knew, who was older than eighteen, male, and of sound body and mind for which the draft was not a major obstacle that had to be managed.

The radiant early-morning California sun shone brightly over Travis Air Force Base as our loaded troop plane touched down in the continental United States. The groggy group quietly applauded and, with the opening of the doors, inhaled the sweet fresh air, and bustled down the ramp with a mixture of cheers, back-slapping, and tears. Several kissed the tarmac.

Hardly a one had reached his twenty-first birthday.

The evidence of our year was now on our chests—rows of battle ribbons indicating wounds, heroism, and, above all, dedicated service. It seemed so pure at that moment. So simple. We had served. We had defended liberty on freedom's frontier. We would now receive the kudos of a grateful nation and purposefully get on with our lives.

But there were no crowds.

There were no parades.

Perhaps, we thought, all of that would come later.

So all waited.

Several million of us.

It never came.

Our group quickly scattered. Some stayed to make connecting flights to new duty stations or home. Others boarded troop buses for the Oakland or San Francisco airports. There were hasty good-byes among new friends from the flight, along with promises to stay in touch, but the real parting had occurred days before, in the field, when the extraordinary Charlie Company bonds that had been forged over the past year had been broken—most forever.

I was to be processed for discharge over the next several days at
the Treasure Island naval base in San Francisco Bay. I called and
woke my sister Ruthie who was living in San Francisco with her
husband and newborn daughter, Gretchen. My brother, Don,
was there as well, having come out to greet me and, no doubt,
send reports back to Brookline on the state of my mental and
physical health. Ruthie said they would come pick me up, but it
would take several hours to get there.

Now what?

Alone, weighted down by my seabag, I slowly walked outside of the now-deserted terminal building and found the section
of curb that was closest to San Francisco.

I sat.

The sun grew warmer on my back as the first hour elapsed in
silence. There was not a soul in sight. My senses were overcome,
working in an overloaded state to reprogram my brain to its
new reality. Most apparent at first was the silence—the deafening silence. For nearly a year, there existed an explosive norm of
noise coming from twenty-four-hour-a-day bombing, outgoing
and incoming artillery, choppers—constant choppers—and the
everyday sounds made by two hundred fifty boys living in very
close quarters.

Now there was silence.

I tried to return my mind to the present, but the past became
more awful with each fleeting recollection—images of the hundreds of grotesque enemy bodies still splayed across LZ Loon
the day we returned, their bodies fragmented from the bombs
and charred by the napalm; the long patrols through fetid rice
paddies and suffocating air that offered no relief. I remembered
drinking canteens full of swamp water flavored with halazone
purification tablets and Kool-Aid, and the smoky stench of
burning human waste.

The future seemed inconsequential by comparison.

Now I was alone.

Completely alone.

There was a moment on LZ Loon, during a brief lull on the third day when we all knew the end was before us, that I felt fear for the first time—raw fear for my life. I remember wishing desperately at the time that I could disappear—evaporate. Who would know the difference? I was one marine in a country of hundreds of thousands. My presence was inconsequential to the overall fight against encroaching Communism.

Real abject fear.

Now alone on the curb, I began to shake and cried for the first time.

And cried.

Another hour passed while I waited for Ruthie to make the drive out from San Francisco. I stood occasionally to stretch my legs while gazing down the long base approach road for the sight of a car—any car. The road was empty. The sun grew hotter, but the generated heat was unusually dry and felt most comforting. Ever so slowly the memories again began to dull. Increasingly there was little room for them within the sensual assault I was experiencing.

Would I remember?

I took solace in the fact that I had written so many letters home. They would be my record. My memory.

I would not read them again for more than thirty years.

Neither would I cry again, for thirty years.

....

An oddity of the Vietnam War was that most combat participants did not go over or return as a unit. That had been the case with Charlie Company and me. I showed up on a Tuesday, one of three to report that day, and left on a Friday, the only one to leave. I flew over with a planeload of boys from all branches of the service who were assigned to dozens of different units upon arrival. Months later, I returned home with another group with whom I had no common bond, other than the war from whence we came. Few, if any, marines arrived and departed together.

Although there was only one way for a United States Marine to enter Vietnam, there were three ways to leave. He could come home safely by plane, as I had just done. He could come home in a body bag as so many of my Charlie Company comrades had already done and would continue to do long after I arrived home. The third way home was a medical evacuation after a stay in Delta Med in Dong Ha, one of two hospital ships off the coast of Da Nang, or after a stay in the United States Naval Hospital in Japan. Wayne Wood, Doc Mac Mecham, and dozens of the LZ Loon wounded returned in this manner. We rarely ever saw a seriously medevaced marine again. We'd hear rumors about their location or the extent of their wounds, but most never returned to the field.

While waiting in front of the Travis terminal, I remembered Mike Kilderry. We had affectionately dubbed him Snowball because of his white-blond hair and bright-eyed demeanor. When the first rocket hit LZ Loon, Snowball and I were sitting on the side of our fighting hole smoking a cigarette. We ducked when the round hit, but a tiny piece of shrapnel caught the lower right part of his back, just below his flak jacket. He had a corpsman look at it, and then returned to grab his gear. He was being medevaced for what appeared to be a nothing injury. Minutes later when he arrived at Delta Med in Dong Ha, he was unconscious. He was immediately transferred to another helicopter and flown to the hospital ship *Repose* off Da Nang.

On July 6, 1968, Mike Kilderry, one of the sweetest souls to ever walk the earth, died.

Those of us who returned standing up came home one by one and evaporated into the country. Each was left alone to fight his own private war, and face a country that was tired of the war and openly antagonistic to those veterans who'd fought in it. I did not have to be called a baby killer more than once to know that to openly discuss my military service in civilian circles in 1968 was a terrible idea.

....

At long last, a lone dark blue Chevrolet Malibu sedan made the approach to the terminal. Donny was driving with Ruthie also in the front and Gretchen sleeping in her car bed in the back. Ruthie later remembered me as "standing there tall, handsome, and healthy, and looking a bit tentative."

There we were—loading my seabag into the car—gazing at one another from head to toe, wondering what to say, trying to find the words and emotions to fit a moment that had no precedent in our young lives—an epic family event being shared for the first time by three siblings with no parents in sight.

All that was Marine Corps or Vietnam flew from me like water off a shaking dog.

I climbed into a car for the first time in a year.

I rolled the window down and turned the radio up. As we headed for the freeway, I stuck my head out and let the sweet cool air fill my lungs over and over again. The regular morning commuters looked at me with curiosity. They had no idea.

Their daily routine was just beginning.

My new life was just beginning.

In San Francisco the climate was very antiwar. I was coming from nine months fighting in it, while most people there had spent the nine months fighting against it.

After calling my parents, I immediately called the Oakland naval hospital in hopes of locating Doc Mac Mecham. Oakland was the amputee center for boys who hailed from west of the Mississippi. The Philadelphia naval hospital covered the East.

Doc was there and thrilled to hear my voice. He was largely recovered from the physical wounds from the LZ Loon blast that had cost his right thumb, and, since he was a navy corpsman, he had been put on a regular shift at the hospital while awaiting his eventual discharge from the navy. I could have no understanding of his fermenting mental wounds, to say nothing of my own.

Later that day, he drove over to San Francisco in his red Austin Healey and picked me up at Ruthie's house in the Sunset District. We then shot back across the Bay Bridge to Oakland and the hospital, with the top down and the Chambers Brothers' "Time Has Come Today" playing at full volume on the little car radio. Dustin Hoffman re-created the scene in *The Graduate*— top down across the Bay Bridge to the music of Simon and Garfunkel.

I could not imagine there ever being a more wonderful moment in my life.

Minutes later, we pulled up to the cavernous old facility and parked.

As with so many other events over the past two years, there was nothing in my experience that could possibly have prepared me for what I was about to face on that gorgeous late July afternoon.

I had bought a box of fresh doughnuts. I hadn't known what else to do.

Our footsteps echoed as we walked down the long white-washed hallways past a seemingly endless number of partially open doors that revealed the human remnants of other eras— navy and Marine Corps veterans from distant wars, either dying from injuries sustained long ago or just dying.

We turned the final corner and pushed open the frosted double doors that contained the amputee ward. All of the boys in the room had recently sustained their injuries in Vietnam. After being medevaced from combat, most had spent days or weeks being stabilized on a hospital ship offshore before being moved back to the States. Once in Oakland, they remained a month or two to be fit with prostheses, undergo physical therapy, and just lie there contemplating their new lot in life. As we were a mere seven weeks removed from the horror of LZ

Loon, there was an inordinate number of marines from Charlie and Delta companies lying prone between the crisp white sheets of the beds in the amputee ward of the Oakland naval hospital.

There was nothing in my life's experience that could have provided balance or perspective to that which flooded my eyes as I gazed down the dimly lit ward. The human detritus of our three days on LZ Loon was spread before me. How could I possibly connect what my eyes observed with what my brain could rationally process?

It was horrifying.

The first person I came to was Wayne Wood. We had joined Charlie Company during the same week the previous November. He had been a machine gun squad leader. He wasn't supposed to have been, but his predecessor had been killed shortly before we'd arrived and a replacement had been needed. Woody had gotten the job. If I'd been first into the command bunker that day, I would have gotten the job.

After that first week, the next time I saw Woody, he had an M60 machine gun carefully balanced on his right shoulder with seven bandoliers of NATO 7.62 ammo hanging around his shoulders. Put a knife in his mouth and he could have passed for Pancho Villa. He had just celebrated his eighteenth birthday and had a sixteen-year-old girlfriend named Jan back home in Iowa. At every opportunity over the seven months, he'd pull out Jan's dog-eared picture and speak incessantly about their love and impending marriage. Occasionally we'd avoid him because of it. We could all recite the story almost verbatim.

Shortly after the first rockets hit on the fifth of June, the Skipper called for volunteers to bring the wounded up to the LZ to be medevaced. Woody jumped from his hole and ordered his squad to action. The next round killed them all.

Except Woody.

The rocket from Co Roc, Laos, exploded and sent a sickening monsoon of metal through the leaves and elephant grass. The larger pieces screamed by unaerodynamically until cracking into a tree trunk, thudding into a mound of red clay, or ever so quietly slicing off the skinny pink leg of a seventeen-year-old boy. The smaller pieces sounded like a downpour of rain, with every drop being lethal cargo.

Wayne Wood was thrown fifty feet by the explosion and became filled to overflowing with the full complement of large and small shrapnel. It is difficult to imagine a person alive with more metal in his body than Wayne Wood. His screams haunted me for years. Here he was now in the amputee ward of the Oakland naval hospital without a leg and filled with enough shrapnel to make his every breath a miracle.

I had been blown over by the concussion from the same round that June 5 and had been completely covered with dirt. The larger pieces had either missed me or stuck in my flak jacket. Hundreds of the microscopic ones had filled the unprotected area of my upper arms and neck. For nearly fifteen years afterward, tiny shards from that one round eventually rose to the surface of my skin. One by sickening one, I'd pull them out with tweezers.

That same round had also wounded Doc Mac Mecham, who had been providing field triage to the wounded that Woody and his squad had been ferrying to the LZ.

Incredibly, Woody spent the twenty-minute flight to Delta Med in Dong Ha fully conscious with more pain in more places than could ever be inventoried. He was immediately transferred to the hospital ship *Repose* off Da Nang.

Doc Patterson was there in the amputee ward as well.

Patterson had been hit by rifle fire on the morning of June sixth, with me close by. He'd been crouched over a wounded marine. I watched in horror as a bullet entered his knee, traveled up his thigh, and exited through his pelvis. His face was frozen in shocked disbelief. The expression haunted me for years. Doc Patterson had been in country for less than one week.

Here they all were, filling bed after bed of this ward and most of a neighboring ward.

This did not include boys who were sent to Philadelphia.

Doc Mac and I stayed for an hour and then headed back across the bay.

As he dropped me off, we vowed to get together again before I left.

We didn't.

It would be thirty-seven years before we met again.

27

DAYS LATER I WAS DISCHARGED FROM ACTIVE DUTY. It was a beautifully bright early afternoon when I emerged from the out-processing center, clutching my DD-214 and drinking in the breathless view across the bay.

Freedom!

All seemed right with my world.

Hours away would be the homecoming in Boston of which I had dreamt for months.

I was wearing the summer khaki uniform that had been issued almost two years before, during my final days at Parris Island. Although I had gained several pounds over the previous week, the uniform still hung loosely from my shoulders and hips. The weight of the ribbons and metals on my chest made the left side of my shirt hang noticeably lower than the right. The diet of C rations and swamp water had taken its toll.

Ruthie came to pick me up for the last time and drove me to the San Francisco airport for the flight home.

Later that night, after boarding the half-loaded plane, I noticed that I was the only one in uniform. Most of the other passengers looked through me as though I weren't there. They didn't know that I was going home and had no way of knowing what the medals on my chest represented. To them I wasn't even a curiosity.

Stewardesses were different—always friendly, solicitous, and eager to give a first-class upgrade when available. Many could spot a homecoming veteran across the tarmac. Most troop flights in and out of Vietnam were on commercial air carriers—complete with airline food and movies. The stewardesses would drop off a planeload of nervous eighteen-year-old boys in Da Nang at two o'clock and leave with a load of exhausted battle-weary veterans an hour later. Incredible in retrospect. On the next day they would do it again. The following week, they might be back on domestic routes dealing with business travelers.

In several weeks, I was to become the first Vietnam veteran to enter Harvard University. I would then become unique in a not very good way. Student dissent against the Vietnam War was rising to a crescendo on college campuses around the country in the fall of 1968. It was not a good time for a returning marine to publicly express pride in having served his country in harm's way. It was, in fact, a bad time.

Throughout the night of the six-hour flight, thoughts of Dan Burton and the boys of Charlie Company slowly and inextricably faded as I began to contemplate the reality of my life ahead. By the time the plane landed, I had pushed much of the experience out of my consciousness into a deep bottomless well, from whence it would not begin to bubble up for another twenty-five years. My brother-in-law Jim Lizotte later described my Vietnam experience as an impenetrably dense little pellet deep within me to which no one, including myself, was permitted access.

Early the next morning the plane lowered through the clouds and began its final approach across Boston Harbor. Gazing with wonder at the changing skyline, I noticed the singular clock tower of the old Custom House and shook my head. My memory took me back to the clutch of five boys huddled around Sergeant Miller's desk in the first-floor recruiting office nearly two and a half years before, with our right hands held high and our hearts filled with pride as we enlisted in the United States Marine Corps.

I wondered at that moment where the other four were—indeed, where Sergeant Miller was. One or two of them were certainly dead. I remembered the hundreds of boys in their underpants wandering from station to station around the cavernous Boston army base, while being subjected to their pre-induction physicals. Where were they? Across the nation, throughout the years of Vietnam buildup, that scene was repeated thousands of times as millions of boys were processed. In the end, nearly sixty thousand would not come home alive.

We landed and slowly taxied to the gate. As the door opened, I could feel the heavy humid New England summer air ooze into the cabin. We filed down the steps, onto the tarmac, and across to the gate area, where my parents were craning to see my head among our group. I was very happy to see them. The greeting included a quick kiss from my mother and a handshake from my father. They were all smiles, as were several neighboring people who added handshakes and back pats when they realized the nature of this homecoming.

I was home.

Alone.

My mind was on the future. I couldn't wait to get out of my uniform and on with my life. Minutes later, the seabag in my hand, we headed for the car and made the short drive through the tunnel, down Storrow Drive, and home to Brookline. We dropped Dad off at his office in Kenmore Square on the way. When Mom and I arrived at our house, I was tired and relieved.

It was eight o'clock in the morning.

The early light poured into our house as I dragged my heavy seabag in the back door, completing the final leg of its long journey. Mom made me a breakfast of bacon, eggs, toast, orange juice, and coffee. The two of us spent the next hour at the dining room table making some small talk but mostly just quietly looking at each other in disbelief.

As my last feeble spasms of energy began to flicker, I pulled my seabag to my side, retrieved several personal items from the top, closed it, and dragged it down the cellar stairs to the far corner of the basement, where it remained untouched for years. I climbed back up to the kitchen, kissed my mother on the cheek, walked up the two flights of stairs to my room, removed my uniform for the last time, and collapsed onto the crisp clean sheets that waited on my gently turned-down bed.

I was asleep before my head hit the downy fluff of the pillows.

The following morning—or perhaps it was later that same day—jet-lagged, culture-shocked, and still exhausted, I took my parents' big green Plymouth Fury out the gravel driveway and down High Street to navigate the twenty-five miles up Route 93 to Andover. Barby was finishing a six-week course at the Andover summer session. I was going to pick her up.

Every conceivable memory and emotion coursed through my veins during the forty-five-minute drive north. I was disoriented after my sleep but still felt my new life gaining on me with a speed for which I was ill prepared. Memories of other drives up to Andover—the deep depression of a new winter term or the day so long ago when my mother first drove me up from Summit to begin my freshman year—flashed in and out, all overlaid with the unscratchable itch of wondering what Dan Burton was doing at that moment. What hill was Charlie Company on? What time was it on the DMZ?

Had I really actually just been in a war?

A fucking war?

Barby had been the most vulnerable participant in the awful family drama that had unfolded over the past year and was, thereby, the one whose welfare had continually caused me concern. She hid it from me well. Any piece of correspondence from her absolutely made me smile, no matter the heat, the wet, or the horror of the moment.

It had been a long dark year for the three on the home front.

After I returned, I realized that they had all lived under a nine-month cloud at 14 Allerton Street. Each morning, they anxiously checked the *New York Times* front page for any news of Charlie Company. On June 15, their nerves were jangled when the photograph of our body snatch did in fact make the front page of the *Times*—above the fold.

Evenings brought the *CBS Evening News with Walter Cronkite*. Vietnam increasingly and predictably became the lead story there as well. Every Thursday, Cronkite would read the weekly body count. Dozens turned to hundreds turned to thousands during 1968. The family's dinner table talk was always about what they'd heard of the war, reading my old letters aloud, checking the map of Vietnam that was hung in the downstairs bathroom to see exactly where I was. Wondering why I hadn't written that day.

Barby said later, "It was scary thinking you might be killed, and it put a pall over everything. An unspoken gloom. Sitting in the darkened living room as the projector hummed and we saw slides of you and your buddies and the bunker, et cetera. 'What do you suppose that is,' Mom would say to Dad as they tried to decipher the slides without you to give a narrative. It was quite a time."

And suddenly there I was, turning off Main Street onto Chapel Avenue and the Andover campus. Pulling to a stop, I looked up the familiar path that wound through the tall pines to Henry L. Stimson House. Then I saw Barb walking—and then running—down the path after catching sight of me at the wheel of the family car. It is a sight that will forever remain deeply etched in my mind's eye. Had I picked a moment to cry, that would have been it.

But I didn't.

There was nothing of my year away that would evoke such a deep emotion again for another thirty years.

28

SEVEN YEARS LATER, DA NANG FELL.

On a Tuesday evening in early April, I was driving toward home down the Brooklyn-Queens Expressway from my job as the assistant ticket manager of the New York Mets at Shea Stadium. I turned on the car radio and heard the news. The enormous American combat base that I'd first seen from the window of a banking Pan Am 707 in October 1967 was quietly taken over by the army of North Vietnam. It had been abandoned by the United States days before. Actually, it had been turned over to the Army of the Republic of Vietnam (South Vietnam) for safekeeping.

Da Nang. Jesus.

I remembered all of the activity: marines, napalm-laden jet fighters taking off every thirty seconds, hundreds of people wandering around the enormous PX as though they were in a Sears store in Grand Rapids, wiry pasty-white boys with bronzed necks and lower arms enjoying a two-day in-country R & R at China Beach, *big* guns, hundreds of tanks, enormous ammo dumps, huge petroleum tank farms, and the steady daily flow of munitions and material being directed in country from the sprawling United States Marine Corps supply center in Barstow, California.

Da Nang.

For the first time in seven years, I actually thought about Vietnam for more than a few minutes. During my two years in the Marine Corps, I had written home nearly every week. The night that I heard that Da Nang had fallen, I felt a need to write one last letter home.

Brooklyn, New York
April 1975

Dear Home,

Horror, chaos and anarchy—Da Nang, spring 1975. And so it now begins as it ends. The light at the end of the tunnel is a dark one. As the end is certainly inevitable, I am touched for the first time in seven years at seeing it occur.

The C-2 bridge, Gio Linh, indeed Con Thien, and hill whatever are as strategically significant now as Waterloo, Verdun, Gettysburg, Dien Bien Phu, all now dots on a map surrounded by placid countryside inhabited by a generation which appreciates it only as history, spoon fed without the emotional scars of the ravishing reality that is war.

So now may the American era of Vietnam become History.

The mothers alone shall continue to ask "Why?" with a perspective that does not tolerate the antiseptic analyses of historians. The mothers shall continue to chronically grieve for the Sid MacLeods with fervor far beyond their control. Indeed, as arthritis reacts to a rainy day, so shall they be agitated by the sight of refugees fighting for non-existent hope as the noose tightens upon the sacred soil their sons bled upon. The mothers like their sons shall soon die.

I am sad that Vietnam went the way it did, but in a country run by politicians, it fell characteristically, apathetically.

We gave a weak body a false high so many years ago and last week, after the addict had reached a multimillion dollar a day habit, the supply was cut off—no public stances, no firm policy decisions—indeed it occurred through the absence of any decision. As the body began to shake with withdrawal, the pusher was far away enjoying spring recess at home with family and constituency, struggling for his tenuous tenure on national economic issues seemingly so far removed and yet so directly attached to that horror they created long ago.

The question I have rarely, if ever, addressed myself to in these letters is why—again why? It is fortunately a question I was never forced to answer while I was there. I was called in a time of national need. I served my country with immense pride to the best of my ability. I was discharged. The war was wrong, but this is not an issue for the soldier. "I think . . ." "You are not paid to think."

Soon after, I knew how wrong it was; perhaps I knew while I was there, but it was my first war and I had nothing to compare the phenomenon with. Every soldier who served in that war should share my pride, for we served. Blue Star mothers should not feel bitterness for the loss of their sons, for they served.

We have from this war corporals and captains who may stand on equal elevation with their peers who trod upon the beaches of Normandy—the purpose was to serve. The shame, the bitterness, and the disgust we must feel is for our country which year after year after year ignored its people, betrayed its conscience, and grossly miscalculated its ego by using force, terror, and unprecedented belligerence, while trying to impose a way of life and government that abhors these very same things.

We must publicly proclaim our national guilt. We made a mistake. Is it so shameful to admit that we are human beings?

Rather than sulk in our mire as this nightmare painfully ebbs outward with the tide, we must learn to rule by example. Our books, our minds, our resources are for the world to admire and share if we keep our own house in order and our own sense of rightness and grandeur in perspective.

May we never again forcibly impose with grenades and guns and grand young sons what we tried to impose upon the people of South Vietnam.

Love,
Jack

29

THE THREE WEEKS BEFORE CLASSES BEGAN BECAME infamously marked in American history. On August 8, 1968, Richard M. Nixon successfully overcame challenges from former New York governor Nelson Rockefeller and former California governor Ronald Reagan to gain the Republican nomination for president during the party's quadrennial convention held in Miami Beach. The following evening, Spiro T. Agnew of Maryland accepted the nomination for vice president. Both would eventually resign in disgrace, victims of their own dishonesty and the ongoing war in Vietnam.

On August 20, the Soviet Union invaded Czechoslovakia with more than two hundred thousand troops, putting an end to the so-called Prague Spring, and began a period of enforced and oppressive "normalization."

On August 26, while the Democratic party reluctantly nominated Hubert H. Humphrey for president at its convention in Chicago, thousands of students outside the hall were noisily protesting the war in Vietnam and the inability of the American political process to stop it.

Without provocation, the Chicago police stormed the crowd, injuring more than one hundred people before a live worldwide television audience. The protesters were chanting "The whole world is watching" for the international media that was filming. The following day, while speaking at a news conference, Mayor Richard Daley uttered the malapropism that became a symbol of the times: "The policeman isn't there to create disorder; the policeman is there to preserve disorder." Daley was such an unwittingly galvanizing force that the statement perhaps defined the moment when opposition to the war in Vietnam became institutionalized in the United States.

Memorial Hall is one of the older structures on the Harvard University campus. It is a cavernous edifice of dubious architecture that was built in 1878 to commemorate those Harvard alumni who died (for the Union) during the Civil War. It was being used this day as a center for freshman registration.

The entrance hall was huge, drafty, and dimly lit. Upon its dingy old paneled walls were engraved the names of the dead, arranged by order of graduating class. This was the first war memorial that I had seen since returning. I wondered if Sid or Snowball would ever have their names carved on a memorial. I hoped so, but it didn't seem likely. Those dead inscribed on memorials were older—our parents' age or older—not kids like us. Besides, our war wasn't like World War II or the other big ones. There didn't seem to be any sentiment to remember those who'd died in Vietnam.

It became increasingly obvious during my brief month back that Vietnam was not a war Americans would choose to celebrate in the grand tradition of the great wars. Would Harvard later commission a noted architect to design a monument such as this to the sacrifice of her grand young sons who had served in Vietnam? It seemed unlikely.

Indeed, few sons of Harvard would ever serve, let alone die, in Vietnam. Elite colleges had become a sanctuary from military service because of the draft laws that allowed students to "defer" military service for the term of their attendance. To ensure that

status for ensuing generations, Harvard, and many other colleges, eliminated on-campus ROTC the following year to protest America's involvement in the Vietnam War. Thus began an
enormous schism between the military and the country's centers
of higher learning. This continues largely unchanged to this day.

Harvard had admitted me, but there was little if anything
about the institution that was friendly to veterans of the Vietnam War. I knew that I had earned my place, but I would never
feel respected by my class or the institution for my achievement
of the previous two years. Those precious few who were curious
about my time in the Marine Corps dwelled more on their complete inability to understand why someone like me ever would
have enlisted in the first place. Mostly my Vietnam service rarely
came up. When it did, I was not the initiator.

The interior of Memorial Hall was more akin to a Gothic
cathedral than a university building. High above, great wooden
arches dwarfed the interior. Entering exterior light was refracted
through dozens of enormous stained-glass windows. Before me
was stretched the length of a football field of folding tables
manned by a cross section of university life, including athletic
teams, academic and social clubs, and volunteer organizations
and antiwar groups.

Hundreds of voices echoed off the walls and then echoed
again—then again. The discordant cacophony was disorienting
and grated on my every nerve. The occasional loud noise still
made me flinch and would instantly take me back to Vietnam. It
could take minutes for me to recover my composure. Noises really rattled me—to a large degree, they still do. The involuntary
responses for my survival that had been so finely honed were not
as easily buried as the memories of the experience.

I was approached by all manner of hawkers eager for my
participation in their chosen extracurricular area. It had elements of a bazaar. The rowing coach took particular interest,
given my height and muscularly lean frame.

The students all looked young. How was I ever going to fit

in? Not even ninety days had passed since the horror of LZ
Loon—less time than most of these students had just spent on
summer vacation.

After a bewildering several minutes of absorbing the frenetic
scene, I was directed to a corner table over which was displayed
a sign with the letters K–P. I stood briefly in line and then recited
my name to the person behind the table and was given a fat
manila envelope that contained registration materials.

My name was typed boldly on the outside.

No service number.

No rank of corporal.

Just my name.

Unlike how I felt on my first day at Andover, I now felt that
I belonged and had earned my way through the front door as
surely as if I had gotten 800s on my College Boards. I had little
concern that the academic difficulties I had faced at Andover
would follow me. I'm pleased to report that they did not.

I registered for courses in the areas required for freshmen
that included the full range of liberal arts disciplines. There
would be no Care and Cleaning of the M60 Machine Gun with
Sergeant Rodriguez here. The college pep band wandered
through the building playing fight songs. One such, "Ten Thousand Men of Harvard," was composed to raise the blood of the
faithful on the football field against Yale—not exactly "The
Marines' Hymn," but then again, Yale wasn't exactly the North
Vietnamese Army either.

It all seemed simply manageable.

Almost quaint.

Later that afternoon I was sitting on the steps of the Fogg Art
Museum prior to an orientation session. A lovely girl sat on a
step nearby. Nervously, I took a deep breath and opened.

"Hi."

She turned slowly, as though lost in thought. "Oh, hi," she
responded.

"Are you here for the orientation?" I continued.

"Yes."

"Where are you from?" I asked. She didn't appear to be particularly responsive.

"Connecticut. Ethel Walker," she answered. Ethel Walker was an all-girl prep school outside of Hartford. She did not ask about me, so I stumbled forth anyway.

"I'm from here—well, near here—Brookline. I went to Andover." This was going nowhere. I felt as though I were in a battle with neither a rifle nor training. I was devoid of all social skills. This was tough.

"Andover?" She lit up suddenly. "Did you know Freddy Witherspoon? He went to Andover too. I met him last summer on the Cape."

"Well, no. I mean, well, his name sounds familiar. He would have been a sophomore when I graduated." Now what? I thought. Might as well come out with it. "I actually graduated from Andover two years ago. I've been serving in the United States Marine Corps for the past two years. I just got back from Vietnam."

"Oh."

That was it. "Oh."

No "How great it must be to be home."

No "Thank you for your service."

No "You're a fucking baby killer."

No "I've always wanted to do it with a marine."

No nothing.

Just "Oh."

With that, she rose and headed up the steps into the building. The conversation, such as it was, was over. I had learned a valuable lesson. Few, if any, people at Harvard cared about military service—particularly Vietnam service. From that point on, for the next four years, and well beyond, I barely mentioned it.

30

IN NOVEMBER WE RETURNED TO ELIZABETH, NEW Jersey, for the Thanksgiving celebration with Grandma and Grandpa. After Grandpa completed the recitation of his annual poem, he asked the entire family to hold hands and stand in a circle with me in the center. He was proud of what I had accomplished and was relieved that I was home safe. Upon his command, all sang three verses of "When Johnny Comes Marching Home." I felt self-conscious at first but drew increasing strength by looking at Grandpa. He openly cried as he sang. I had never seen anyone shed an actual tear over my service.

This was my homecoming parade. It was the only formal recognition I received for my service from any quarter.

By the end of 1968, there was nothing at all pleasing about being identified as a veteran of the Vietnam War—even among family. We veterans had become the physical symbols of our nation's gross military misfortune. Our returning status was the polar opposite to that of our fathers, a brief twenty-three years before, who had returned from Europe and the Pacific to universal adulation and appreciation.

It was relatively easy for me to push Vietnam out of my mind—school started, I had books to read, papers to write, and I began to very awkwardly socialize with friends and girls. There was nothing in Brookline or Cambridge to trigger even the vaguest memory of my previous year—no military bases, no marines, no jeeps, no jets, no incoming artillery, not even any short hair. Most important, perhaps, it was hard to even find anybody who cared that I or any other American serviceman had served his country in harm's way. If I didn't bring up the subject, the subject didn't come up.

I didn't bring up the subject.

As long as I could stay away from the *CBS Evening News with Walter Cronkite,* Vietnam existed only as the object of increasingly passionate protest rallies on and around American college campuses.

I could not, however, push Sid MacLeod out of my mind.

Day and night his memory haunted me—as it does to this day. Sid.

I just didn't know what the hell to do.

I found his old address and wrote a clumsy note to his mother and father. I didn't know what to say. Here I was, alive and safely in college—exactly where he had been three years before when he'd gotten the bright idea to enlist in the United States Marine Corps. What made it a conundrum was that, like me, he'd enlisted voluntarily. Unlike me, however, he had really wanted to serve in Vietnam, and now he was dead.

Dammit.

McLean, VA
December 2, 1968 (Friday)
Letter from Lillie and Sid MacLeod

Dear Jack,

We wanted you to know how much we appreciated your letter. I fully intended to write sooner but kept putting it off; I still find it quite difficult to write about Sid.

He did mention you to me several times and told me
what a good friend you were. I'm sure he admired you as
much as you did him.

We have only the fondest and loving memories of Sid. He
was an inspiration to us, his parents, as well as to others. We
could not have asked for a finer son.

We hope all is well with you and that you are now back
to the routine of civilian life again.

Thanks again for taking the time to write. I know how
difficult it must have been for you.

We wish you the best of luck in the New Year.

Sincerely,

Mrs. S. MacLeod

EPILOGUE

MY TRANSITION INTO ACADEMIC LIFE WAS NEARLY seamless. I had a number of classmates from Andover who were now juniors and were able to give me a good base of support and guidance where appropriate. (Stay away from Econ 201, whatever you do.)

I lived at home for the first semester, so I was able to study with few distractions. I quietly slid back into family life as well. Activity around the Brookline household returned to what I knew as normal. There was little, if any, talk about the previous year. By November, I had without fanfare or ceremony taken down the map of Vietnam that had hung on the downstairs bathroom wall.

In the late afternoon when I got home from classes, Barby and Mom would be sitting in the parlor having their daily "Tea and Beav," that is, watching *Leave It to Beaver* on TV while having afternoon tea. Sometimes when Mom picked up the mail from under the mail slot in the vestibule, she would quietly sing to herself the refrain, "Oh, dear. No mail from John today."

To me these were mere words. To Barby and, of course, Mom, they were echoes back to a year of awful afternoons and wrenching weeklong silences cut by the relief—the enormous relief on those days when a letter came in—of knowing that I had at least been well five days before. I have no earthly idea what that must have been like for the three of them back in Brookline and can no more imagine their experience than they could mine. To them, the clang of the vestibule mail slot was akin to a sniper's single rifle shot.

Every day.

By June, I had finished a successful freshman year, moved onto campus, and felt the strange relief that came from knowing that every boy that I had served with in Vietnam was now either safely home or dead.

On a raw late March New England day three and a half years later, a thin manila envelope addressed to me arrived through the vestibule mail slot in Brookline. The return address was the Department of the Navy in Washington, D.C. My mother picked it up along with the other mail, sorted out what applied to her, and put the rest in the gold tray on the front hall table. I would come by, perhaps, over the weekend, for a home-cooked meal and a break from my studies.

It was spring term of my senior year at Harvard University. This time the thin envelope contained good news. On March 29, 1972, my six-year obligation (two on active duty and four in the inactive reserves) was complete. I was honorably discharged, at the rank of corporal, from the United States Marine Corps.

In the meantime, I had quietly morphed into one of those Columbia University types that had evoked such visceral reactions from my Charlie Company buddies years earlier.

To the world I now appeared to be just another "long-haired, privileged little shit-fuck draft-dodging motherfucker."

Except for the draft-dodging part, of course.

ACKNOWLEDGMENTS

This book emerged from more than one hundred letters home that I wrote during my two years in the United States Marine Corps from 1966 to 1968. My mother saved the letters and often encouraged me to "do something with them." Thirty-five years later, my second wife, Karen, discovered the letters, as deeply buried among my possessions as my Vietnam War experience was buried inside of me. Karen echoed my mother's earlier encouragement.

I began writing.

Thank you, Karen, from all of us.

Through fellow author, marine, and Vietnam veteran Bob Timberg, I met my agent, Flip Brophy of Sterling Lord Literistic. Flip introduced me to my editor, Katie Hall. Katie's remarkable talent washes unseen over every word on every page. Flip also encouraged Ryan Doherty of Random House to bring the work to life. There would be no *Loon* without each of them. Thank you.

While writing, I received encouragement and support from family, friends, neighbors, professional colleagues, and fellow Charlie Company survivors in an abundance that I continue to regard with awe. Terry and Nancy Tillery kept me focused by providing food, love, and unlimited access to their beach house in Kill Devil Hills, North Carolina. In Georgetown, Vera and Dandy Dickie were my daily visitors, keeping me sane with an encouraging word and a welcome wag. Thank you.

Former Charlie Company commander Bill Negron was a font of information. Many technical details are from his memory, and several of the better stories were borrowed with his blessing from his own writings. Bill, a uniquely American character, was a remarkable marine, and a dear friend to all of us. Thanks, Skipper.

Among Charlie Company veterans, I thank Dan Burton, Mac Mecham, Jack McQuade, Robert Rodriguez, Benny Lerma, Buck Willingham, Doug McPhail, Clabie Edmonds, Neil Downey, Wayne Wood, and Gaylord Flippen. Semper Fi, brothers.

For support in Washington, I thank former marines Peter McCarthy and John Miller, as well as John Shlaes, Tad Howard, Tom Coleman, Peter Van Allen, David Mitchell, and author David Maraniss. Andover classmate Ray Healey was a steady cheerleader. Ray never served in the military, but has dedicated his life to veteran advocacy. Thanks from all of us, Ray.

My three daughters and three siblings were unconditionally supportive rocks throughout the entire process. Thank you Sarah, Martha, Sylvia, Don, Ruth, and Barbara.

Present in spirit and never to be forgotten are the forty-three grand young sons of Charlie and Delta companies, 1st Battalion, 4th Marines, 3rd Marine Division who breathed their last on LZ Loon during those three horrific days in June 1968.

Rest in peace, brothers.

The third of four children, JACK MCLEAN was born in Huntington, New York, on May 26, 1947. He was brought up in Summit, New Jersey, where he lived until admittance to Phillips Academy, Andover, at age fourteen. Upon graduation, McLean enlisted in the United States Marine Corps. After boot camp and a year of stateside duty, he served in Vietnam with Charlie Company, 1st Battalion, 4th Marine Regiment, 3rd Marine Division.

McLean returned to enter Harvard University in the fall of 1968 as the college's first Vietnam veteran. After graduation, he held marketing positions in New York, Boston, Maine, North Carolina, and Washington, D.C.

McLean is the father of three daughters and is currently the Tsien Writer in Residence, Fort Lee, New Jersey.

Printed in the United States
by Baker & Taylor Publisher Services